THE SHARED TABLE

VEGETARIAN & VEGAN FEASTS TO COOK FOR YOUR CROWD

By Clare Scrine

Photography and design by
Savannah van der Niet

For my family, friends and dear housemates.
Thank you for sharing your lives and your tables.

And to all those who find their joy in cooking.

CONTENTS

WHAT A PLEASURE IT IS TO SHARE A TABLE!

I'M A FIRM BELIEVER IN THE POWER OF SHARED MEALS TO BRING PEOPLE TOGETHER, BUILD FRIENDSHIPS, AND CREATE COMMUNITIES.

Yes, it's a little corny, but sharing a meal is the easiest excuse to catch up with old friends, housemates, and family. It makes sense to me that such meals should be lovingly prepared and as delicious as possible. I think a shared table is the best place to passionately discuss the state of the world, and sometimes—for a small moment—to escape it. I wrote this book to celebrate those times, and hopefully encourage you to have a whole lot more of them.

This book was particularly inspired by my own experiences living in sharehouses, and the intense, wonderful connections I have created with so many housemates. Cooking and sharing food with my current housemates is one of our main sources of connection. We actively try to make our house a space where others are regularly invited for a shared meal. The recipes are designed to suit this environment—that is, you can scratch together many of these dishes with mostly pantry staples and a few cheap additions and still feed a large crowd.

Food has always been my language of love. Cooking a meal for someone can be such a clear way of showing care. From 10 years old I've cooked for those I love nearly every day and night. Cooking, for me, is a self-taught skill, finely tuned over more than a decade in more kitchens than I can count. Over that decade, the act of cooking for others has been a source of connection with people all around the world.

Some people find solace from their stress, loneliness, or existential crises in art, music, dancing, or travel. For me, cooking has always been my outlet. Cooking is something I can (almost always) have complete control over. It's a task I know I can do with ease. Cooking now requires so little brain power that it's purely a therapeutic and creative outlet.

The driving force behind this project has always been to share my feelings about the power of sharing food and to put something into the world that was purely for the joy of it. For as long as I've been cooking, I've been learning that in this big and sometimes painful world of ours, you can never make too many delicious bowls of pasta or raspberry cheesecake brownies to share with your mates. Obviously it's a huge privilege to have the time and resources to cook for others in this way, or simply to cook for pleasure at all, and this is something I acknowledge unreservedly from the outset.

Making *The Shared Table* has been such a wonderful, exciting, and rewarding process. I hope these recipes inspire you to invite around some buddies for dinner, and pause to appreciate just what a joy sharing a meal can be.

ABOUT THIS BOOK

THIS BOOK IS A CULMINATION OF A LIFELONG LOVE AFFAIR WITH COOKING AND SHARING FOOD.

It is my attempt to create a hard-copy record of more than a decade of cooking for family occasions, housemate dinners, birthdays, café customers, get-well-soon drop-offs, activist events and meetings, community barbecues and fundraisers, and simply for myself and those I love. I wrote it in the hope it would be a food sharing guidebook of sorts. It's the resource to consult when you're cooking for a crowd or asked to bring a dish to share. It's a guide to cooking for your community—be they your colleagues, family, mates, housemates or lovers. Sharing food is a joy, but it is also the best way to reduce waste, energy and time spent cleaning and cooking.

So for this reason, this is a book of banquets and big portions. Every single recipe makes a big bowl or plate full of food designed to be placed in the centre of a table, ready to be dug into by the masses.

This book will show you that cooking beautiful food doesn't need to break the bank. Cooking for crowds can be expensive. However, I believe that by cooking in bulk, growing your own, using your freezer efficiently, shopping in season, substituting frequently and using what you have, cooking needn't be an expensive affair. I've found that when cooking on a budget, planning is essential. Using what you already have, writing lists, and checking for easy substitutes will prevent wasting food and money. This book is designed so that each feast contains similar types of food and key ingredients, so that you can make lots of different things out of the same core ingredients.

This book is also an ode to shared homes. It's a snapshot of my friends' and my own lives in sharehouses. The eight chapters were shot in different locations throughout the inner suburbs of Brisbane, mostly in different friends' sharehouses. Most meals were conceptualised, tested and perfected within a sharehouse environment, and *The Shared Table* endeavours to capture the warmth, affection, and unique connection of a loving house, as well as the role that shared meals have in creating and nurturing this. By shooting and writing recipes with these people in mind, this book also becomes a celebration of my home city, Brisbane (Meanjin). It captures some of the most beautiful parts of this city, its slow pace, incredible weather and strong sense of community.

This isn't a health book. Most of the food is really healthy, but some of it is full of sugar or oil. I believe in balance in food and I try and refrain from thinking of food purely as fuel, or medicine, or as the key to health. The recipes are all vegetarian and many are vegan, or have easy vegan substitutes. I am not a hyper-strict vegetarian or vegan. I don't buy or cook meat myself for environmental reasons. I think there are fundamental problems with all industrial production of animal products. I also don't think that individual choices about consumption will solve these problems, nor will everyone we know becoming vegetarian fix the climate crisis. I digress. What I am trying to communicate is that this book is for everyone. For meat-lovers, strict vegans, and for everyone in between.

This is a book made possible by the incredible creative talent and generosity of friends and strangers. *The Shared Table* was made possible by the blind faith and support of people who bought copies online before I had a single recipe written. Every single dish or ware you see photographed has been loaned by an independent artist or potter, or it has been loaned by a friend or family member. Failing that, it's been sourced second-hand from op-shops.

COOKING RULES I LIVE BY

I HAVE ALLUDED TO SOME OF THESE WITHIN PARTICULARLY RELEVANT INTRODUCTIONS TO SOME OF THE RECIPES IN THE BOOK. HOWEVER, MOST OF THEM GO UNSPOKEN, YET ARE ALWAYS RELEVANT.

- Bigger is almost always better. My recipes make large portions, and I often double them. If you're not cooking for a crowd, most of them will keep well for leftovers.

- If unsure, use more olive oil. And if you're going to invest in one good-quality item, make it olive oil.

- Same goes for garlic—if you're unsure, use more. On a similar note, people love garlic bread (heavy on oil and garlic). When in doubt, I always make some to add to a meal.

- Substitute ingredients according to what's going cheap at the markets—that's what is in season. I've included suggested substitutes along the way, but get creative.

- Never use pre-made salad dressing. Ever. Just don't do it. My go-to salad dressing: olive oil, a little lemon juice, a little balsamic, garlic and a pinch of salt and pepper.

- When cooking something savoury, make sure you season everything. Doing this as you go is usually best for the overall flavour. For example, when roasting vegetables to add to another dish, lightly season the vegies themselves, then add to the dish and then season the dish as well. If you taste something and it doesn't wow you, add a dash of salt. It's often the secret ingredient that's missing in vegetarian cooking.

- Grow herbs and use them without reserve. I use fresh herbs in almost every recipe in this book and I never measure quantities.

- Buy in bulk. Bulk-food stores or big deli outlet-style shops often sell big, cheap bags of ingredients like nuts and spices. Store them well in sealed jars. You'll save heaps of money and can avoid shopping at mega supermarkets.

COOKING RULES
I LIVE BY
Continued

- When you roast vegetables, don't just cook them to soften them. You want them in a hot enough oven, and for long enough, that they shrivel and darken in colour. That's when they take on that heavenly flavour.

- Rinse your tomato tins with a little water (or wine) and throw it into whatever sauce or dish you're making.

- Always reserve a little pasta cooking water to add to your sauce before tossing the pasta through.

- When frying or sautéing, stop stirring your food so much—especially when making sauces and curries. Vegies browning and sticking to the pot a little is good; that browning is where the best flavour is.

- Similarly, when frying vegetables, don't overcrowd the pan. Just as you wouldn't cook a heap of steaks in together, don't load bucketfuls of mushrooms into a frying pan and expect them to caramelise and colour.

- Once you have the confidence to do so, cook lots of things at once. I tend to do a big Saturday cook-up most weekends and make 4–5 dishes at a time. I love cooking this way because it reduces the amount of energy, time and effort significantly, and you only have to clean up once. Plus, if you're a busy person, it is a major time saver.

SOME PRACTICAL NOTES

THE SHARED TABLE IS STRUCTURED AROUND EIGHT BANQUET-STYLE MENUS FOCUSING ON A PARTICULAR TYPE OF MEAL.

The dishes in each chapter all complement each other, but they are also complete meals in themselves. Each chapter is tied together by core components, a similar theme and style of food. Non-pantry staple ingredients tend to be repeated frequently within each chapter. This is intentional! The chapters are designed so that you and your loves could prepare the whole banquet for one special meal and not need to buy an extreme quantity of things. Of course, each recipe is also perfectly wonderful on its own.

Writing recipes is challenging for me because I struggle to *follow* recipes at the best of times. I believe in cooking by intuition, by taste and by feel. Of course, for someone who spends less time cooking than me, this may be somewhat intimidating. Nevertheless, I would encourage you to embrace flexibility, taste as you go and trust your instincts when cooking my recipes—do not be afraid to change things up.

Feel free to swap ingredients (use Google if you need to), and don't feel you need to measure everything precisely—especially seasoning, herbs and spices. Taste everything as you go so you become familiar with how flavours come together, and feel free to go a bit rogue.

Making mistakes when cooking is where you'll develop skill, by learning what works and what doesn't. Many delicious things have been invented off the back of an averted disaster.

SOME PRACTICAL NOTES

Continued

QUANTITIES, ESPECIALLY WHEN IT COMES TO THE SIZE OF VEGETABLES, BUNCHES OF HERBS AND SEASONINGS, WILL VARY.

Use your best judgement and keep the essential rules on pages 13–14 in mind as you do. Here are a few general notes, though.

- A 'bunch' of leafy herbs—basil, coriander (cilantro), mint, parsley—generally equates to about 2 full handfuls of leaves.

- A tin of tomatoes, beans, coconut milk etc. are all a standard 400 g (14 oz) tin.

- Unless stated, 'diced' refers to a 1 cm (½ inch) dice. Finely diced is about 2.5 mm (⅛ inch).

- All vegetables generally suggest a medium size, so you'll need to adjust your quantity depending on the size of the produce. If the recipe calls for two eggplants (aubergines), but there are only very small eggplants at the shop, use extra.

- Olive oil always refers to extra virgin. Olive oil quantities are used loosely as a guide. I never, ever, measure olive oil.

- Oven temperatures do vary. Know your oven and adjust the temperature and cooking time using your best judgement.

- All tablespoon measurements use a regular 20 ml (¾ fl oz) measurement. All cup measurements refer to a regular 250 ml cup (8½ fl oz/1 cup). Adjust accordingly if using US measurements.

You'll find at least one or two of the following notes at the top of nearly every recipe:

- *Vegan or vegan option* – this dish is either vegan or can be tweaked to be made vegan with a few simple substitutions or omissions.

- *Gluten free or gluten-free option* – this dish is gluten free or can be tweaked to be made gluten free with a few simple substitutions or omissions.

- *Leftovers friendly* – this dish is just as good, if not better, the next day or so. Store the cooled dish, covered in the fridge, for up to 3 days.

- *Freezer friendly* – this dish can be put in a sealed container and frozen for up to 3 months. Ensure the dish cools completely before it is packaged up in a reusable container and frozen.

A SHARED KITCHEN

This book is designed with a sharehouse in mind. My sharehouse has a large, communal pantry, which we all contribute to. We buy everything that keeps well—like grains, legumes and tinned goods—in bulk, so they're always on hand. Our fruit and vegies are mostly shared too, so we buy bulk basics that keep well communally, and then each buy our more specific items ourselves. Sharing a kitchen in this way means we shop less and waste less. It also means there's always something to make for dinner.

UTENSILS

I have a well-stocked set of cupboards filled with various kitchen gadgets. I would recommend just three as essential:

A good-quality food processor

This could be a standing blender or a stick blender with different attachments. Esential for making dips, blended soups and sauces, and helping to chop vegetables in bulk.

A set of hand-held beaters

I've never really seen the need for a super-expensive bench mixer, but a simple hand-held set of beaters will come in mighty handy for baking and whisking.

A grill press

These are designed to make toasted sandwiches on—which of course is great. However, I also use mine to grill vegetables or tofu almost every day. They're super efficient and cook with a really high heat, which ensures incredible flavour.

PANTRY STAPLES

Everyone's pantry and kitchen will be stocked a little differently, and by no means needs to be this comprehensive. Below are the essentials we always have on hand, which form the bulk of the ingredients required for recipes in this book.

Baking

almond meal
baking powder
bicarbonate of soda (baking soda)
coconut (desiccated and shredded)
flour (plain/all-purpose and self-raising)
golden syrup
honey
nut milk
peanut butter
sugar (brown, icing and caster/superfine)
vanilla extract (natural)

Bases and Bulkers

black beans (tinned and dried)
breadcrumbs (regular and panko)
chickpeas (tinned and dried)
coconut milk
kidney beans (tinned and dried)
lentils (red and brown, tinned and dried)
noodles (soba and rice vermicelli)
pasta (lasagne sheets, spaghetti,
    penne, spirals, macaroni)
polenta (quick cooking)
rice (basmati and brown)
semolina
tinned tomatoes
tomato passata
    (puréed tomatoes)
TVP (textured
    vegetable protein,
    dried)

Spices and Flavourings

basil (dried)
bay leaves
cardamom (ground and pods)
caraway seeds
chilli flakes and sauce
Chinese five-spice
cinnamon (ground and sticks)
coriander (ground and seeds)
cumin (ground and seeds)
curry pastes
fennel seeds
oregano (dried)
paprika (sweet and smoked)
sesame oil
soy sauce
tahini
turmeric (ground)
vegetable stock powder or cubes
vegetarian oyster sauce
 vinegars (white, red, rice wine and
    apple cider)

Fruit, Nuts and Seeds

almonds (slivered and whole)
chia seeds
currants
dates
peanuts
pepitas (pumpkin seeds)
pine nuts
sesame seeds (white and black)
sunflower seeds
walnuts

Bench Essentials

black pepper
extra virgin olive oil
garlic
sea salt
table salt
vegetable or sunflower oil for frying

Fruit and Vegetables

apples
bananas
carrots
eggplants (aubergines)
leafy greens (spinach, rocket, kale)
mushrooms
onions
potatoes
pumpkin (winter squash)
sweet potatoes
tomatoes
zucchini (courgettes)

Chapter One

A BREAKFAST SPREAD

Blakeney Street

BLAKENEY STREET:
A BREAKFAST SPREAD

The first meal of the day is often a solitary and simple affair. These recipes are for those occasions that deserve a shared feast first up—a birthday, holiday, or social Sunday morning. This menu has a few breakfast classics and some more unusual fare. This breakfast spread was devoured by Han, Steve, Dan and I, in Han and Steve's home. Their place is a super-cosy, one-room studio apartment in the Brisbane suburb of Highgate Hill, with the most incredible morning light.

Vegan Muffins

Shakshuka

Bagels with 'Everything' Topping and Zesty Vegan Cream Cheese

Herby Haloumi and Zucchini Fritters

Avocado, Cucumber and Sesame Salsa

Honey Roasted Macadamia Dukkah

VEGAN MUFFINS

This is your perfect basic muffin recipe, ready to add whatever flavourings, fillings or toppings your heart desires. Pictured here is one batch with an extra banana, a cup of oats subbing in for ½ cup flour, ½ cup chopped nuts and a teaspoon of ground cinnamon. The other batch has ½ cup raspberries and 2 teaspoons of rosewater added. Whatever flavour I make these muffins, I always like to add something on top, even if it's just a sprinkling of sugar. This helps create a classic crunchy top and looks lovely.

Makes 12 small muffins • vegan, leftovers friendly, freezer friendly

INGREDIENTS:

1 large banana, mashed

1 tsp natural vanilla extract

170 ml (5½ fl oz/⅔ cup) vegetable oil (sunflower, canola, peanut are all good too)

250 ml cup (8½ fl oz/1 cup) non-dairy milk of choice (soy, coconut, oat or almond)

170 g (6 oz/¾ cup) caster (superfine) sugar

375 g (13 oz/2½ cups) self-raising flour

Flavour Ideas

80 g (2¾ oz/½ cup) grated carrot, 1 tsp ground cinnamon and ½ tsp ground allspice for carrot cake muffins

chopped strawberries

peanut butter swirled through the batter

passionfruit pulp and shredded coconut

dark chocolate and nuts

oats and cinnamon, topped with maple syrup

1 tsp rosewater, ½ tsp ground cardamom and 65 g (2¼ oz/½ cup) chopped pistachio nuts

METHOD:

Preheat the oven to 180°C (350°F). Line a regular 12-hole muffin tin with baking paper, or grease with a little oil or margarine. (If your muffin holes are large, you should have enough batter for about eight muffins.)

Place the banana, vanilla, oil, milk and sugar in a large bowl and whisk together.

Add any desired flavours and stir well.

Add the flour in two batches, stirring gently until it is just beginning to combine. It's ideal to be able to see a little flour throughout the mix, as this gives a great texture. Do not overmix, or your muffins will become chewy.

Spoon the mixture into the muffin holes. Bake for 15 minutes, or until golden on top and just cooked through the centre.

SHAKSHUKA

Shakshuka is the perfect thing to make your breakfast a little bit special. This recipe is fairly traditional except for the addition of Persian feta, which creates these incredible pockets of salty flavour. For a beautiful sauce, really sizzle the heck out of the vegetables when you're frying them—don't be afraid of letting them brown, or even blacken in parts. The trickiest bit of the dish is ensuring you don't over or undercook your eggs: remember, they will continue to cook in their own residual heat after being removed from the oven. A cast-iron pan or ovenproof frying pan is perfect here, but if you don't have one, you can transfer the sauce to a baking dish before adding the eggs. Double or triple the recipe to feed a larger crowd.

Serves 2–3 • gluten free

INGREDIENTS:

2 tbsp olive oil

1 small red onion, thinly sliced

1 small capsicum (bell pepper), thinly sliced

2 ripe tomatoes, diced

2 garlic cloves, crushed

1 tsp cumin seeds

1 tsp smoked paprika

1 tsp ground coriander

400 g (14 oz) tin chopped tomatoes

4–6 eggs

50 g (1¾ oz) soft Persian feta

1 handful parsley leaves, chopped

METHOD:

Preheat the oven to 180°C (350°F).

Heat the olive oil in an ovenproof frying pan. Add the onion and capsicum and fry over high heat for about 10 minutes, tossing the vegetables every minute or so. Add the fresh tomatoes, garlic and spices. Reduce the heat to low and cook for another few minutes.

Add the tinned tomatoes, a splash of water and some salt and pepper, then simmer for about 10 minutes, until thickened.

Make some little spaces in the sauce with a spoon and gently crack the eggs into them, carefully spooning a little sauce over some of the egg white. Sprinkle with salt and pepper.

Transfer to the oven and bake for 6–7 minutes, or until the egg whites are just beginning to set. Remove from the oven and gently crumble blobs of feta all around the dish. Return to the oven for a final minute or two of cooking.

Remove from the oven and sprinkle the parsley over before serving. Best eaten warm, with plenty of fresh toast to mop up the sauce.

BAGELS WITH 'EVERYTHING' TOPPING AND ZESTY VEGAN CREAM CHEESE

Bagels are a total rip-off to buy, but so cheap and satisfying to make yourself. If you feel like loading up your freezer, double or triple the recipe and simply bag up the cooked and cooled bagels, then defrost and eat as needed. Making bread in any form always seems a bit arduous the first time, but gets easier and is so worth it when the final product is a success. These bagels are my favourite, sprinkled with a classic 'everything' topping—but feel free to substitute at will using the seeds and spices you have at hand. You can also add different toppings such as cheese or herbs, and fillings like sun-dried tomato, spring onion (scallion) or jalapeño chilli. The nuts for the cream cheese need a few hours soaking, so plan ahead.

Makes 8 bagels and 2 cups cream cheese • vegan, leftovers friendly

BAGELS WITH 'EVERYTHING' TOPPING AND ZESTY VEGAN CREAM CHEESE

INGREDIENTS:

2 tsp active dried yeast (1 × 7 g sachet)

1½ tbsp sugar

375 ml (12½ fl oz/1½ cups) warm water, approximately

600 g (1 lb 5 oz/4 cups) strong white bread flour, plus extra for dusting

1½ tsp salt

3 tbsp nut milk, or 1 beaten egg white

'Everything' Topping

1 tbsp poppy seeds

1 tbsp sesame seeds

1 tbsp garlic flakes

1 tbsp salt

cracked black pepper, to taste

Vegan Cream Cheese

115 g (4 oz/¾ cup) raw cashew nuts

250 g (9 oz) firm tofu

zest of 1 lemon

2 tsp lemon juice

1½ tsp apple cider vinegar

¾ tsp sea salt

1 tsp caster (superfine) sugar

3 spring onions (scallions), very finely chopped

75 g (2¾ oz/½ cup) capers, drained and chopped

1 handful chopped dill

METHOD:

In a small bowl, combine the yeast and sugar with 100 ml (3½ fl oz) of the water and leave for 5 minutes. Meanwhile, mix the flour and salt in a large bowl and make a well in the centre.

Add the yeasted water to the flour with about half the remaining water. Mix together, adding the remaining water as needed to form a firm, moist dough.

Turn the dough onto a clean, floured surface and knead for about 10 minutes, adding more flour as needed to form a dough that is smooth, elastic and firm.

Place the dough in a clean, lightly oiled bowl, turning it to coat, and cover with a tea towel. Let the dough rest in a warm place until doubled in size, about 1 hour.

Using floured hands, push the air out of the dough. It should shrink back to its original size. Set aside and let it rest for another 10 minutes.

Meanwhile, preheat the oven to 180°C (350°F) and line a baking tray with baking paper. Combine all your 'everything' ingredients in a small bowl and set aside.

Cut the dough into eight pieces. Dust your hands with plenty of flour and gently mould each dough portion into a smooth ball. Try to pull the crinkles to one spot at the bottom of the ball, and pinch them together. Make each ball into a ring by poking your finger through the middle and working it to stretch the bagel to your desired size and shape. Let the bagels rest for a few minutes while you bring a large saucepan of water up to the boil.

Using a slotted spatula, carefully lower each bagel into the boiling water. Poach for 2–3 minutes, turning each one over at least once. Remove the bagels and drain off the excess water.

Transfer the drained bagels to the lined tray. Brush each bagel with nut milk (or egg-white glaze) and sprinkle generously with your 'everything' topping. Bake for 20 minutes, or until golden.

TO MAKE VEGAN CREAM CHEESE:

Put the cashews in a bowl and cover with about 3 cm (1¼ inches) water. Set aside for at least 2 hours, or preferably overnight.

Drain the soaked cashews of all excess liquid and place in a high-power blender. Add the tofu, lemon zest, lemon juice, vinegar, salt and sugar. Add 2 tablespoons fresh water and blend for 1–2 minutes, starting on low speed, then increasing to high after 30 seconds. The mixture is very thick, so make sure you use the tamper to move the ingredients around, to ensure they all blend.

Once the mixture is thick and everything is blended together, transfer to a bowl. Add the spring onions, capers and dill and combine with a spoon. Taste and season further if desired. Store in the fridge until you're ready to smear it all over your bagels. The cream cheese will store in the fridge for up to a week.

Note: This vegan cream cheese is delicious, but you can really only make it if you have a proper high-power blender with a tamper (a stick to move the ingredients around). Instead, you could add the lemon zest, spring onions, capers and dill to 300 g (10½ oz) pre-made cream cheese (vegan or otherwise).

HERBY HALOUMI AND ZUCCHINI FRITTERS

These fritters are a really quick and easy way to escape a routine toast-based brekkie.
They're delicious served with sour cream and chutney, with chilli sauce, on their own, or as part
of a brunch spread—however you like! I love them with eggs, rocket (arugula), avocado and
hollandaise sauce. They're even pretty good cold the next day.

Makes about 15 fritters • gluten-free option, leftovers friendly, freezer friendly

INGREDIENTS:

3 medium zucchini (courgettes),
grated

250 g (9 oz) haloumi, grated

½ bunch dill, chopped

½ bunch mint, chopped

3 spring onions (scallions),
finely chopped

zest of 1 lemon

1 tbsp lemon juice

3 eggs, whisked

100 g (3½ oz/⅔ cup) self-raising flour
(or gluten-free flour)

1 tsp salt

100–200 ml (3½–7 fl oz) olive oil,
for pan-frying

METHOD:

Put all the grated zucchini in a colander. Sprinkle liberally with salt and let it sit
for 10 minutes.

Rinse the salt off, then squeeze all the water out of the zucchini; this is essential for
crispy fritters. Pat dry with a clean cloth.

Transfer the zucchini to a bowl and add all the remaining ingredients, except the
cooking oil. Stir well to combine.

Heat a large frying pan with a big glug of olive oil, enough to cover the pan by at
least 5 mm (¼ inch). Once the oil is sizzling hot, add the fritter mixture in heaped
tablespoon quantities.

Allow each fritter to fry until golden brown underneath (about 1–2 minutes), then
flip. Press them down slightly to ensure the middle is cooking. Reduce the heat and
cook for a further 2–3 minutes. Transfer to a plate.

The fritters are best served fresh and hot, but are easily brought back to life in a
frying pan or warm oven once chilled.

Note: I grate the zucchini and haloumi using the grating attachment of a food
processor, which makes it incredibly easy. A box grater will do fine, though.

AVOCADO, CUCUMBER AND SESAME SALSA

Lovely and light, this is a beautiful way to eat your morning avocado. The salsa is a little bit special, with a Japanese influence, and is a great side for lots of other meals—say on top of a cold soba noodle salad, or next to some teriyaki tofu, but I also love it for breakfast on toast with a fried egg. Make this dish vegan by swapping the mayo for a vegan version. Conveniently, there's a recipe for a quick and easy vegan mayo on page 52.

Serves 4–6 as a side • vegan option, gluten free

INGREDIENTS:

1 tbsp sesame oil

1 tbsp rice wine vinegar

1 tbsp soy sauce

1 tsp caster (superfine) sugar

½ red onion, very thinly sliced

2 ripe avocados

1 small Lebanese (short) cucumber
(or one-third of a telegraph/continental cucumber), halved lengthways, then sliced into very thin half-moons

1 tbsp white sesame seeds

1 tbsp black sesame seeds
(or more white sesame seeds)

2 tbsp Kewpie mayonnaise

1 tsp wasabi paste

METHOD:

Combine the sesame oil, vinegar, soy sauce and sugar in a small bowl. Add the onion slices and mix well to ensure every piece is separated and coated in the marinade. Set aside for 10–15 minutes.

Meanwhile, halve the avocados and remove the stones. Cut the flesh into 1–2 cm (½–¾ inch) pieces and place in a bowl, along with the cucumber.

Warm a frying pan over low heat and add the sesame seeds. Cook, stirring for a few minutes, until the white seeds begin to turn golden brown. Add a pinch of salt and set aside to cool slightly.

Scoop the onion out of the marinade and add it to the avocado mixture. Add the mayonnaise and wasabi paste to the remaining marinade and whisk well to combine. Taste and season with salt and pepper to your liking.

Add most of the toasted sesame seeds to the avocado mixture and toss gently to combine. Drizzle the sauce over the avocado mixture and gently fold to coat.

Transfer to a serving bowl and top with the remaining toasted sesame seeds.

HONEY ROASTED MACADAMIA DUKKAH

I love having a jar of homemade dukkah handy on the kitchen benchtop. It's such a lovely way to spice up a simple meal. This delicious dukkah is perfect atop avocado toast, most salads, or sprinkled over poached eggs or roasted vegetables. It's a wonderful addition to so many meals, and oh-so-lovely with some good bread and olive oil. This is a great base recipe, but you can swap out the nuts or spices for whatever you have on hand and experiment with different flavours once the basic method is down pat.

Makes about 1 cup • vegan option, gluten free, leftovers friendly

INGREDIENTS:

100 g (3½ oz/¾ cup) macadamia nuts

115 g (4 oz/¾ cup) almonds, pistachios or walnuts (or a combination)

1½ tbsp honey (or maple syrup)

2 tsp ground pepper

1 tbsp fennel seeds

1 tbsp cumin seeds

2 tbsp sesame seeds (a mixture of black and white, if possible)

2 tbsp coriander seeds

METHOD:

Preheat the oven to 180°C (350°F).

Arrange the nuts on a baking tray. Drizzle the honey evenly over the top and sprinkle generously with salt.

Roast for about 8 minutes, or until the nuts are golden and toasted and the honey is bubbling and dark brown. Remove from the oven and allow to sit on the tray for 10 minutes to cool.

Meanwhile, toast the spices and seeds in a clean, dry frying pan over low heat for 4 minutes, stirring often.

Transfer the nuts and spices to a food processor. Pulse until finely chopped, but not powdered. Add salt to taste and pulse once more. Taste the dukkah again and add more seasoning if desired.

Transfer to airtight containers or jars. The dukkah will stay fresh for several weeks.

Chapter Two

HANGOVER BRUNCH

Princhester Street

PRINCHESTER STREET:
HANGOVER BRUNCH

A big night often begets a big hangover, and a big hangover in our house is often soothed by a big, greasy and very slow brunch. This menu is filled with all the components that make up my ideal big brunch spread, heavy on carbs, oil and simple, hearty flavours. The recipes were shot on a perfectly rainy day in my own sharehouse, a massive haven in West End, featuring housemates Issy, Mon, Harriet, Fynn and Rose.

Tray-Baked Leek and Potato Hash Brown

Slow-Baked Beans

Scrambled Tofu and Sizzled Capsicum Tacos

Easy Vegan Pancakes with Quick Berry Compote

Baked Chilli Mushrooms

Egg, Kale and Haloumi Hand Pies

Apple and Beetroot Relish

TRAY-BAKED LEEK AND POTATO HASH BROWN

What kind of hangover is not remedied, or at least helped, by a good load of oily, salty potato? My head feels clearer just thinking about it. I have made some variation of this tray-baked hash brown for a bunch of worse-for-wear mates more times than I care to think about. I love the fried leeks and spring onions, which add a subtle sweetness. If you're really organised, you can cook the potatoes the night before, which will ensure the best starchy consistency. I like this hash best when topped with a fried egg or some apple and beetroot relish (see page 60).

Serves 6–8 • vegan, gluten-free option, leftovers friendly

INGREDIENTS:

1 kg (2 lb 3 oz) starchy potatoes (I use russets)

vegetable oil, for pan-frying and drizzling

1 small leek, washed well and thinly sliced

4 spring onions (scallions), thinly sliced

1 large handful dill, chopped

110 g (4 oz/¾ cup) plain (all-purpose) flour (or gluten-free or corn flour)

2 tsp salt

METHOD:

Load the potatoes into a large pot and fill with hot water. Bring the water to the boil and let the potatoes cook for a further 10 minutes. Drain and set aside until cool enough to handle.

Meanwhile, preheat the oven to 200°C (400°F). Line a baking tray with baking paper.

Heat a frying pan with a splash of vegetable oil over high heat. Add the leek and spring onions and cook for 5 minutes, stirring every minute or so. Set aside.

Grate the potatoes using a food processor or box grater. Combine the grated potato in a large mixing bowl with all the remaining ingredients. Taste and add extra salt and pepper if desired.

Press the mixture onto the lined tray. Rough up the top with a fork and drizzle with a little extra oil and extra salt (to ensure the top crisps up).

Bake the hash brown for 30–40 minutes, or until the top is deeply golden and crispy. Allow to cool slightly, then cut it into squares, or just scoop portions onto everyone's plates to serve.

SLOW-BAKED BEANS

By cooking the beans both on the stove and in the oven, they develop a super-rich, tomatoey flavour. Baking them also crisps up the top layer, providing a great contrast with the mushiness underneath. Forget those sickly sweet tinned baked beans (kidding, they are obviously still delicious and should never be totally ditched). These are a little more special. Make 'em for a big brekkie spread, or just on a slow Sunday to eat on toast throughout the week. I love them with a side of greens and polenta for dinner, too.

Serves 6–8 as a side • vegan, gluten free, leftovers friendly, freezer friendly

INGREDIENTS:

2 tbsp olive oil

1 brown onion, diced

2 garlic cloves, crushed

1 tsp dried rosemary, or 1 small handful fresh rosemary, chopped

200 g (7 oz) cherry tomatoes, diced, or 4 ripe roma (plum) tomatoes, diced

2 × 400 g (14 oz) tins cannellini beans (including soaking liquid)

2 × 400 g (14 oz) tins good-quality tomatoes (I use cherry tomatoes)

1 tbsp sugar

1 large handful fresh basil, chopped, plus extra to serve

METHOD:

Preheat the oven to 160°C (320°F).

Heat a frying pan with the olive oil and add the onion. Cook over medium heat, stirring occasionally, for about 5 minutes.

Add the garlic, rosemary and fresh tomatoes, and a pinch of salt and pepper. Cook for a further couple of minutes.

Add the beans (including their soaking liquid), tinned tomatoes and sugar. Reduce the heat and cook for about 10 minutes, until simmering.

Transfer the mixture to a baking dish and stir the basil through. Taste and add more salt and pepper if desired. Bake for 40–60 minutes, or until the mixture is thickened and browning on top, stirring once halfway through cooking.

Serve sprinkled with extra basil.

Note: Butterbeans are a great substitute for cannellini beans in this recipe.

SCRAMBLED TOFU AND SIZZLED CAPSICUM TACOS

This combo of curried tofu, smoky capsicum, sharp pickled radish, fresh coriander and creamy mayo is heavenly. These tacos work well on their own, or as part of a spread. They're something a bit different for brekkie, and just as good for lunch or dinner. I like to finish mine with some chilli sauce and a squeeze of lime.

Makes 12 tacos • vegan, leftovers friendly

INGREDIENTS:

1 tbsp sugar

1 tbsp white vinegar

3 radishes, halved and thinly sliced

80 ml (2½ fl oz/⅓ cup) olive oil

4 capsicums (bell peppers), in mixed colours if possible, thinly sliced

450 g (1 lb) firm tofu

1½ tsp salt

2 tsp curry powder

3 tbsp nut milk

12 small flour or corn tortillas

1 avocado, halved and thinly sliced

1 bunch coriander (cilantro), picked into sprigs

Vegan Mayo

125 ml (4 fl oz/½ cup) soy milk

2 tsp lemon juice

250 ml (8½ fl oz/1 cup) vegetable oil

1 tsp dijon mustard or mustard powder

pinch of salt, to taste

METHOD:

To make the mayo, combine the soy milk and lemon juice in a blender (or emulsify with a stick blender in a bowl) for about 20 seconds. While blending, slowly add the vegetable oil in a very slow steady drizzle, until the oil is emulsified and the mixture thickens. Add the mustard and salt, and continue to blend. Taste and adjust the seasoning to your liking. Transfer to a serving bowl.

In a small bowl, combine the sugar, vinegar and a pinch of salt. Add the radishes and mix well so that each slice is marinating in the pickling liquid. Set aside.

Heat a large frying pan with 2 tablespoons of the olive oil until smoking. Add the capsicums. Cook over very high heat for 7–10 minutes, tossing only every 2 minutes or so, allowing the capsicum to char sightly. Finish with a sprinkle of salt and pepper. Set the capsicum aside in a bowl.

In another bowl, crumble the tofu with your hands. Massage the salt and remaining 2 tablespoons olive oil into the tofu.

Reheat the frying pan, add the crumbled tofu and cook for a few minutes, stirring often. Add the curry powder and nut milk, reduce the heat and cook for a further 3–5 minutes. Taste and add extra seasoning if you like. Set aside.

Assemble the tacos by first heating the tortillas slightly, either in the microwave, in the oven for a few minutes, or just a few at a time in your pan for 30 seconds. In each tortilla, place a spoonful of curried tofu, a few pieces of capsicum and pickled radish, and a slice or two of avocado. Add a drizzle of mayo and finish with a few coriander sprigs.

Best served warm.

EASY VEGAN PANCAKES WITH QUICK BERRY COMPOTE

A chuck-it-all-in and mix-it-all-up affair, these pancakes are incredibly quick and easy to make. Two minutes to mix and ten minutes to fry—satiate that early morning sweet tooth *tout suite*. Fluffy and moist, you'd never know these pancakes are vegan, but if you'd like them less fluffy and thick, add more milk to thin out the batter. You could add chocolate chips or blueberries to the batter, but I love the pancakes plain with this quick compote and some extra maple syrup; ice cream or coconut yoghurt never go astray either. The compote can be made with any berries you like and would work with stone fruit as well. The batter will last a couple of days in the fridge if you want to make a full batch, but just cook a few pancakes at a time.

Serves 6; makes about 12 medium-sized pancakes • vegan

INGREDIENTS:

1 ripe banana

625 ml (21 fl oz/2½ cups) nut milk of choice (I like almond milk)

½ tsp salt

1 tbsp caster (superfine) sugar

1 tsp natural vanilla extract

375 g (13 oz/2½ cups) self-raising flour

vegan margarine, for frying

Quick Berry Compote

450 g (1 lb/2 cups) fresh or frozen berries

zest and juice of ½ lemon

115 g (4 oz/½ cup) caster (superfine) sugar

1 tsp natural vanilla extract

METHOD:

To make the compote, place the berries, lemon zest and lemon juice in a small saucepan over medium heat. Cook for about 5–10 minutes, stirring regularly. Once the berries have broken down considerably, add the sugar, vanilla and 2 tablespoons water. Bring to the boil, then reduce the heat to low and cook for another 10 minutes. Transfer the compote to a bowl to cool.

Meanwhile, mash the banana well in a large mixing bowl. Add the nut milk, salt, sugar and vanilla and whisk well to combine. Add the flour and gently whisk until just combined—it's important not to overmix the batter, so don't worry if there are a few spots where flour is still visible.

Heat a large frying pan with 1 teaspoon of margarine. Once the margarine is bubbling and the pan is searing hot, spoon your pancake mixture in. How much batter you spoon in depends on how big your pan is, how many pancakes you can cook at a time and how big you like your pancakes, so just use your own judgement. The pancakes will be ready to flip once small bubbles appear in the batter. Cook on the other side for another 30–60 seconds, or until golden and cooked through. Repeat with the remaining batter.

Serve the pancakes warm, with the compote spooned over the top, and any other toppings of your choice.

BAKED CHILLI MUSHROOMS

This is probably my favourite way to cook mushrooms: roasted, slightly citrusy and oh-so-juicy. They're a great 'meat alternative' with just about any meal—as part of a brunch spread, in a burger, or sliced and used as a sandwich or omelette filling, or with some mashed potato and beans for dinner. This recipe is for six mushrooms, but double or triple the amount if you're cooking for a crowd or want a container-full in your fridge (you do). You can also use the same marinade on smaller mushrooms; just adjust the number of mushies accordingly.

Serves 6 • vegan option, gluten free, leftovers friendly

INGREDIENTS:

20 g (¾ oz) butter or vegan margarine

2 tbsp olive oil

3 garlic cloves, thinly sliced

3 spring onions (scallions),
finely chopped

1 mild red chilli, finely chopped

1 tsp salt

zest and juice of ½ lemon

6 portobello mushrooms

1 tbsp thyme leaves
(or 2 tsp dried)

chopped herbs such as dill, parsley,
basil or thyme, for sprinkling

METHOD:

Preheat the oven to 180°C (350°F) and line a large baking tray with baking paper.

Melt the butter in a small bowl in a microwave for 20 seconds. Remove from the microwave and add the olive oil, garlic, spring onions, chilli, salt, lemon zest and lemon juice. Season with cracked black pepper and mix together well.

Arrange the mushrooms evenly around the baking tray. Spoon the butter mixture evenly over each mushroom, then scatter the thyme over the top.

Bake for 20 minutes, or until the mushrooms are browned and cooked all the way through.

Serve warm, with fresh herbs scattered over the top.

EGG, KALE AND HALOUMI HAND PIES

These pies are a lovely addition to a brunch spread and are perfect for transporting and eating at any temperature. They're simple but really satisfying, making them a perfect day-after snack.

Makes 8 small pies • leftovers friendly, freezer friendly

INGREDIENTS:

5 eggs

1 tbsp olive oil

2 tbsp chopped sun-dried tomatoes

2 large handfuls chopped kale

2 square puff pastry sheets

100 g (3½ oz) haloumi, cut into 8 small triangles

4 tbsp ajvar, or chutney of your choice, plus extra to serve

sesame seeds, for sprinkling

METHOD:

Preheat the oven to 180°C (350°F) and line a large baking tray with baking paper.

Crack four eggs into a bowl and whisk them. In a small bowl, whisk the remaining egg (to use as an eggwash) and set both bowls aside.

Heat the olive oil in a large, non-stick frying pan. Add the sun-dried tomatoes and kale and cook for a few minutes over medium heat until the kale is wilted, but still bright green. Season with salt and pepper.

Pour the four whisked eggs into the kale mixture and, using a spatula, gently stir so the eggs cook evenly for just 1 minute. Once the eggs are almost cooked, remove from the heat. Sprinkle with some extra seasoning.

Assemble the pies by cutting each pastry sheet into four squares. Place one haloumi triangle on each square of pastry, aligning the corners so that the pastry can fold to form a triangle. Top with 1 teaspoon of ajvar or chutney. Divide the kale mixture between the eight pies and add it on top of the chutney.

Fold over the top half of the pastry on each pie to create a triangle. Use your finger or a fork to press the edges of the pastry together to seal the pies. Lay the pies on the lined baking tray.

Brush each pie with the remaining whisked egg and top with a sprinkling of sesame seeds. Bake for 15–20 minutes, or until the pastry is golden and puffed. Serve the pies at any temperature, with extra chutney if desired.

Note: Ajvar is a blended roast capsicum (bell pepper) dip available from most good grocers. I love these pies with a spoonful of ajvar inside, as it melts into the filling and gives the whole pie a lovely flavour. Any chutney will do if ajvar is not available.

APPLE AND BEETROOT RELISH

Most people have no idea that making chutney is so easy. It's the perfect way to use in-season fruit or vegies, and if you make loads, it will keep in sterilised jars for years. Chutneys like this one also make great cheap gifts. Beetroot relish is an absolute staple food in my sharehouse—we eat it on pretty much everything: atop scrambled eggs, in cheese toasties, and on homemade röstis with sour cream.

Makes about 2 cups • vegan, gluten free, leftovers friendly, freezer friendly

INGREDIENTS:

olive oil, for pan-frying

2 onions, finely diced

1 tsp ground allspice

½ tsp cumin seeds

½ tsp ground cinnamon

5 small beetroot, grated or cut into very small cubes (roughly 3 cups)

1 large apple, grated

80 ml (2½ fl oz/⅓ cup) red wine vinegar or balsamic vinegar

220 g (8 oz/1 cup) sugar

METHOD:

Heat a saucepan with a little olive oil and fry the onions over medium heat for 10 minutes, or until golden. Add the spices and cook for a further few minutes.

Add the remaining ingredients and stir in 375 ml (12½ fl oz/1½ cups) water. Cook for 5 minutes, or until the mixture is thickening and beginning to bubble.

Reduce the heat to low and let the chutney slowly cook for about 1–1½ hours. It's ready when the liquid sticks to a metal spoon, and the beetroot is soft.

Allow the chutney to cool before packing away in sterilised jars for longer storage, or into airtight containers if you're going to eat it all pretty quickly.

Note: You can use the same method to make many different types of chutney. Substitute in about 3–4 cups of chopped onion, capsicum (bell pepper), tomato or grated carrot instead of beetroot, and get creative with the spice additions.

Chapter Three

A LEISURELY LONG LUNCH

Dornoch Terrace

DORNOCH TERRACE:
A LEISURELY LONG LUNCH

This menu is salad-heavy, with lots of lovely, brightly coloured food and delicious offerings, perfect for a long, slow lunch—food best enjoyed on a verandah, or out in the yard. All of these dishes can be served cold or at room temperature, ensuring none of the fuss of a hot lunch (essential during hot summers). In the heart of Brisbane's West End, this beautiful, leafy sharehouse is home to Ruth, Lilly, Rosie and Ned.

Slaw Salad with Crunchy Seeds and Nuts

Vegan Potato and Broccolini Salad

Paneer and Sizzled Capsicum Kebabs with Curried Mango Sauce

Crispy Butterbean Toasts with Sun-dried Tomato Pesto

Pad Thai Salad with Sticky Tofu

Eggplant with Tahini, Pomegranate, Tomato Salsa and Toasted Almonds

Vegan Cinnamon Doughnuts

Cheesecake Brownies with Raspberries

Banana, Tahini and Date Cake with Ricotta Filling

SLAW SALAD WITH CRUNCHY SEEDS AND NUTS

This lovely salad is a light and crunchy accompaniment to a barbecue spread and works well as a side dish with many types of cuisines. It's also great on a sandwich or roll with some grilled vegies or falafel. I love the salty, crunchy seed topping; it's such a simple way to make a slaw more exciting, using common pantry staples—but you could replace the seeds and nuts with other varieties you happen to have on hand. You could also add in grated carrot, shredded kale or other types of cabbage.

Makes 1 large bowl; serves 10–15 as a side • vegan, gluten free, leftovers friendly

INGREDIENTS:

Crunchy Bits

1 tbsp olive oil

2 tsp cumin seeds

3 tbsp sesame seeds

3 tbsp sunflower seeds

3 tbsp slivered almonds

1 tsp salt

Slaw

¼ white cabbage, thinly sliced

¼ red cabbage, thinly sliced

1 small red onion, thinly sliced

½ bunch flat-leaf (Italian) parsley, chopped

½ bunch coriander (cilantro), chopped

Dressing

1 large ripe avocado, flesh roughly chopped

1 tbsp tahini

1 tsp salt

1 tbsp lemon juice

1 tsp white wine vinegar

2 tbsp olive oil

2 tbsp warm water

METHOD:

To make the 'crunchy bits', heat the olive oil in a frying pan. Add the remaining ingredients and cook for 5 minutes over medium heat, stirring constantly. Ensure you watch the ingredients very closely, as they can begin to burn quickly. Set aside to cool slightly.

Combine all the slaw ingredients well in a large mixing bowl.

To make the dressing, blend all the ingredients together in a food processor or using a stick blender. Add salt and pepper, or more lemon juice, to your taste. (You can also mix together by hand; just mash the avocado with a fork first. The dressing won't be as smooth or creamy, but will still taste delicious.)

Drizzle the dressing over the slaw mix and combine thoroughly to ensure every piece is well coated.

Pour about two-thirds of the crunchy bits into the salad, and toss well to combine. Transfer to a serving dish, and sprinkle with the remaining crunchy bits.

Note: If you have a food processor, you can chop the vegies for this salad super quickly using the slicing attachment.

VEGAN POTATO AND BROCCOLINI SALAD

By cooking the potatoes twice and dressing the salad while it's warm, the flavours really soak into the vegies, making this potato salad a world apart from bland mayonnaise-laden versions. The coconut yoghurt gives it a very fragrant flavour. In the same way bacon bits add to a traditional potato salad, a scattering of crispy fried onions finishes this one off beautifully. You can buy these in packets or jars from most bulk food or Asian food stores. The salad can be made ahead of time, though I like it best super fresh and still a little warm.

Serves 8 as a side • vegan, gluten free, leftovers friendly

INGREDIENTS:

500 g (1 lb 2 oz) waxy (boiling) potatoes, cut into 2 cm (¾ inch) cubes

3 tbsp olive oil

1 red onion, thinly sliced

1 bunch broccolini, chopped into 3 cm (1¼ inch) spears

4 garlic cloves, thinly sliced

300 g (10½ oz) coconut yoghurt

2 tsp dijon mustard

zest and juice of 1 lemon

1 small handful chopped dill

1 small handful chopped flat-leaf (Italian) parsley

3 tbsp crispy fried onions or shallots

METHOD:

Place the potatoes in a saucepan and cover with cold water. Bring to the boil over high heat, then reduce the heat to low. Simmer the potatoes for 10–12 minutes, or tender when skewered with a fork. Discard the water and allow the potatoes to cool slightly.

Heat the olive oil in a large frying pan over high heat. Add the onion and sizzle for a few minutes, tossing regularly. Add the cooled potatoes and cook for a few minutes, until some of the potatoes are beginning to turn golden.

Add the broccolini and garlic, along with a pinch of salt and pepper, and turn the heat down slightly. Cook for a further 3–5 minutes, tossing regularly, until the broccolini has turned bright green. Set the pan of vegies aside and allow to cool for 5–10 minutes.

Combine the yoghurt, mustard, lemon zest, lemon juice and plenty of salt and pepper in a small bowl. Pour the dressing over the warm vegetables in the frying pan and gently mix well to combine. Add most of the fresh herbs and mix them in, reserving some to scatter on top.

Transfer the mixture to a serving bowl. Scatter the remaining herbs and crispy fried onions over the top and serve.

PANEER AND SIZZLED CAPSICUM KEBABS
WITH CURRIED MANGO SAUCE

Made in a similar way to ricotta, paneer is a cheese commonly used in Indian, Iranian and Afghan cooking. It works beautifully with the marinade and the flavours in the dipping sauce, but you could also use haloumi instead. The smoky sizzled flavour of these kebabs, paired with this sweet and savoury mango sauce, makes them a delicious vegetarian main. I like to thread them onto metal skewers, which are reusable and less flimsy than wooden ones.

Makes 10–12 skewers • gluten free, leftovers friendly, freezer friendly

INGREDIENTS:

400 g (14 oz) paneer, cut into 2 cm (¾ inch) cubes

3 small capsicums (bell peppers), in any colour or mix of colours, cut into 2 cm (¾ inch) squares

1 large red onion, cut into 2 cm (¾ inch) chunks

olive oil, for cooking

coriander (cilantro) leaves, for sprinkling

Marinade

250 g (9 oz/1 cup) Greek-style yoghurt

thumb-sized piece of fresh ginger, peeled and chopped

3 garlic cloves, thinly sliced

½ red chilli, halved lengthways, then sliced paper thin

2 tsp garam masala

2 tsp cumin seeds

80 ml (2½ fl oz/⅓ cup) lemon juice

75 g (2¾ oz) butter, melted

Curried Mango Sauce

160 g (5½ oz/½ cup) mango pieces

3 tbsp Kewpie mayonnaise

2 tsp dijon mustard

1 tsp curry powder

1 tbsp lemon juice

METHOD:

Combine all the marinade ingredients in a bowl or dish and season with salt and pepper. Add the paneer, capsicums and onion to the mixture and gently coat in the sauce. Cover and marinate in the fridge for at least 30–40 minutes, or up to 24 hours.

Make the curried mango sauce by mashing the mango with a fork until puréed, then mixing to combine with the other ingredients. (Alternatively you can blend all the ingredients using a food processor or stick blender until smooth.) Season to taste and transfer to a small serving bowl.

Thread the vegetables and paneer onto 10–12 skewers, alternating the ingredients.

Heat a barbecue or chargrill pan with a drizzle of olive oil until searing hot. Cook the skewers for 3–6 minutes, until lightly charred in parts, then carefully turn them over and repeat on the other side.

Place the cooked skewers on a platter and sprinkle with salt and coriander leaves. Serve with the curried mango sauce for dipping.

CRISPY BUTTERBEAN TOASTS
WITH SUN-DRIED TOMATO PESTO

These beans are so damn good I sometimes eat them as part of a brunch spread, or just as a snack. They're insanely tasty and so moreish. It's important to use a non-stick pan to cook them in, and to really cook them for a long while; this ensures their crunchy exterior. When serving these little toasts, you could use a jar of ready-made sun-dried tomato pesto if you don't want to make your own, or change it up and make a pesto sauce using basil, rocket (arugula), roasted pumpkin (winter squash) or capsicum (bell pepper).

— Makes 8 pieces • vegan, gluten free —

INGREDIENTS:

8 slices sourdough bread or pane, cut 1 cm (½ inch) thick

3 garlic cloves, sliced in half diagonally

3 tbsp olive oil

Popped Beans

2 × 400 g (14 oz) tins butterbeans, drained well

2 tbsp olive oil

3 garlic cloves, thinly sliced

1 small handful rosemary leaves

½ tsp salt, to taste

½ tsp pepper, to taste

basil leaves, to serve

1 lemon, cut into wedges, to serve

Sun-dried Tomato Pesto

60 g (2 oz/½ cup) walnuts, toasted

80 g (2¾ oz/½ cup) chopped sun-dried tomatoes

125 ml (4 fl oz/½ cup) soaking oil from the sun-dried tomatoes, or good olive oil

juice of ½ lemon

1 large handful basil leaves

METHOD:

For the popped beans, pat the drained beans completely dry using a clean cloth or paper towel. Heat a large frying pan with the olive oil until searing hot. Add the beans and cook for 10 minutes over high heat, stirring every minute or so.

Meanwhile, make the pesto by blending all the ingredients in a food processor with a little salt and pepper until combined, but still textured. (You can also blend the pesto using a mortar and pestle.) Set aside.

Toast the bread slices in the oven or a toaster, using a grill press, or on the barbecue, until they are golden and hardened. Vigorously rub each slice all over with garlic—the rough surface of the toast will act like a grater, spreading the garlic evenly over the toast. Drizzle each slice with olive oil and sprinkle with a little salt and pepper.

Once the skin on the beans is crisping and the beans are becoming golden and firm, add the garlic and rosemary to the pan, along with the salt and pepper. Cook for a further few minutes until the garlic is golden and the rosemary leaves are becoming crisp.

Assemble by drizzling a little pesto onto each toast and topping with a heaped scoop of beans. Finish with an extra drizzle of pesto, a few basil leaves and a squeeze of lemon.

PAD THAI SALAD WITH STICKY TOFU

This beautiful warm noodle salad is loaded with fresh vegies, crunchy nuts and tossed with the most heavenly dressing. Seriously, this dressing is so good that I recommend tripling the amount and having some set aside ready for a last-minute addition to another meal. This salad is packed with healthy stuff, but is so delicious that it still feels like comfort food.

——————— Makes 1 large bowl; serves 2–3 as a main, or 6 as a side • vegan, gluten free, leftovers friendly ———————

INGREDIENTS:

250 g (9 oz) firm tofu, pressed to remove excess water, then sliced into thin strips

olive oil, for pan-frying

80 g (2¾ oz/½ cup) roughly chopped peanuts (or use cashews or almonds)

1 zucchini (courgette), sliced into thin noodle-like ribbons

1 carrot, sliced into thin ribbons

¼ white cabbage, very finely shredded

½ bunch spring onions (scallions), thinly sliced

1 bunch coriander (cilantro), chopped

1 large handful mint leaves, thinly sliced

200 g (7 oz) dried flat rice noodles (sometimes called pad Thai noodles)

Marinade

2 garlic cloves, crushed

juice of ½ lime

1 tbsp brown sugar

1 tsp Chinese five-spice

2 tbsp soy sauce

1 tbsp sesame oil

2 tsp sriracha or other chilli sauce

Dressing

2 tbsp peanut butter

1 tbsp tahini (or extra peanut butter)

juice of 1 lime

2 tbsp soy sauce

1 tbsp fish sauce (or extra soy if you don't use fish sauce)

2 tsp brown sugar

200 ml (7 fl oz) coconut milk

METHOD:

Combine all the marinade ingredients in a bowl large enough to fit the tofu. Season with salt and pepper and mix well. Add the tofu strips and gently coat, then set aside to marinate for at least 10 minutes, or up to 24 hours.

In a large frying pan, heat a splash of olive oil and add the peanuts. Cook over low heat for 4–5 minutes, tossing often, until they turn golden; be sure to watch them very closely, as nuts tend to burn very easily. Season with a little salt and set aside in a bowl.

Gently toss the vegetables and most of the herbs in a large salad bowl, reserving some of the herbs for serving.

Cook the noodles in a pot of boiling water according to the packet instructions until *al dente*. Drain, rinse with cold water and add to the vegetables.

In the same frying pan you used to fry the nuts, heat a splash more olive oil over medium heat until searing hot. Add the marinated tofu, spreading it out as evenly as possible. Cook for 2–3 minutes, or until the tofu is browning and the marinade has become sticky and dark in colour. Turn each piece over and cook on the other side for another 2 minutes. When all the tofu is cooked, add to the salad and gently mix through.

Meanwhile, combine all the dressing ingredients in a small saucepan over medium heat. Whisk until the mixture is beginning to simmer. Taste and adjust the seasoning to your liking. Allow the mixture to cool for a few minutes.

Drizzle the dressing over the salad and combine gently until it is evenly distributed. Scatter the toasted nuts and reserved herbs on top, and add an extra squeeze of lime and sprinkling of chilli if you like.

Note: It's important to slice all your vegetables incredibly thinly. I use a vegetable peeler or a spiraliser to slice the carrot and zucchini, but you could also use a mandoline, or a food processor with a slicing attachment.

EGGPLANT WITH TAHINI, POMEGRANATE, TOMATO SALSA AND TOASTED ALMONDS

I've been making variations of this dish for years now. It always seems to end up on the table at Christmas and is often my go-to 'bring a dish' meal. It's simple, looks incredible and tastes even better. I love this meal best when the grilled eggplant is eaten warm or at room temperature. If you're planning on saving some of the salad to enjoy in the days to come, I'd recommend keeping the salad elements separate, then gently warming the eggplant for serving, and dressing and topping it fresh each time.

In this recipe I have roasted the eggplant on a chargrill pan, but a grill sandwich press does the job wonderfully, too. If you have neither, roasting the slices in the oven until golden and soft will also work. The main aim is to ensure the eggplant is completely soft and golden brown. This is essential for this dish.

Serves 10–15 as a side, or 8 as a main • vegan, gluten free, leftovers friendly

INGREDIENTS:

olive oil, for drizzling

3 eggplants (aubergines), sliced 1 cm (½ inch) thick

Dressing

80 ml (2½ fl oz/⅓ cup) tahini

2 tbsp olive oil

1 tsp salt

2 tbsp lemon juice

125 ml (4 fl oz/½ cup) warm water

½ tsp ground cumin

Salsa

seeds from 1 fresh pomegranate (see Note)

3 ripe tomatoes, cut into 5 mm (¼ inch) cubes

1 small red onion, finely diced

½ bunch mint, finely chopped

½ bunch coriander (cilantro), finely chopped

1 tbsp olive oil

juice of ½ lemon

Toasted Almonds

1 tbsp olive oil

100 g (3½ oz) slivered almonds

¼ tsp salt

METHOD:

Heat a chargrill pan with a good drizzle of olive oil. Add the eggplant slices in batches and cook on each side for about 5 minutes, or until coloured and softening. Sprinkle each piece with a little salt. Repeat until you have cooked all slices well. Arrange the cooked eggplant on a big platter or in a large wide bowl.

Blend the dressing ingredients using a food processor, or whisk by hand until combined; the dressing should be thick, but drizzle-able. Taste and add more salt and pepper if desired.

Combine all the salsa ingredients in a bowl. Season well with salt and pepper.

Toast the almonds in a small frying pan with the olive oil and salt, stirring often for 3–5 minutes, until they're golden brown. Remove from the heat.

Drizzle the eggplant with the tahini dressing, spoon the salsa over and scatter with the toasted almonds. Garnish with extra herbs if you like.

Note: Everyone seems to have a different method for removing the seeds from a pomegranate. Personally, I quarter mine, then submerge it in a bowl of water and pull out the seeds. The white pith will float to the top, the seeds will sink, and you'll be able to just drain the bowl and have all the lovely little red jewels ready to go.

VEGAN CINNAMON DOUGHNUTS

Is there a better treat to enjoy in the winter sunshine than a hot, fresh cinnamon doughnut? These doughnuts are super easy, quick and fun to prepare. They're crisp and a little crunchy on the outside, but pillowy soft in the middle. Sneaking the seeds of a vanilla bean into the traditional cinnamon sugar adds a classy little touch.

Makes 12 doughnuts • vegan, leftovers friendly

INGREDIENTS:

Doughnuts

50 g (1¾ oz) vegan margarine

125 ml (4 fl oz/½ cup) soy milk

2 tbsp vegetable, sunflower or canola oil, plus about an extra 1 litre (34 fl oz/ 4 cups) for deep-frying

250 g (9 oz/1⅔ cups) plain (all-purpose) flour, plus extra for dusting

1½ tsp baking powder

½ tsp sea salt

55 g (2 oz/¼ cup) caster (superfine) sugar

Cinnamon Sugar

1 vanilla bean

230 g (8 oz/1 cup) caster (superfine) sugar

2 tsp ground cinnamon

METHOD:

Melt the margarine in a small saucepan over medium heat, whisking in the soy milk and 2 tablespoons oil until combined.

In a bowl, mix together the flour, baking powder, salt and sugar, then make a well in the middle.

Tip the melted mixture into the well and mix it all together with a fork to form a wet, thick dough. Divide the mixture into 12 portions.

Heat about 1 litre (34 fl oz/4 cups) cooking oil in a deep-sided pan over high heat. Test the oil to make sure it's hot enough by placing a little dough in it. If it immediately sizzles and begins to turn golden quickly, it's ready.

Reduce the heat to medium. Dust your hands well with flour. Working quickly, poke a hole in each ball of dough and use your fingers to shape it into a ring, then gently place it in the oil. Cook four to six doughnuts at a time for 2–3 minutes, or until golden and floating to the surface. Gently turn each doughnut over and cook on the other side until golden. Transfer the cooked doughnuts to paper towels or a clean cloth to drain.

Meanwhile, make the cinnamon sugar. Halve the vanilla bean lengthways and scrape out the seeds. Crush the seeds and half the sugar using a mortar and pestle, then place into a large bowl with the remaining sugar and the cinnamon. Mix well.

After they've cooled slightly, coat each doughnut in the cinnamon sugar. They are best enjoyed warm.

Note: These doughnuts are meant to be pretty rustic in appearance, so don't worry too much about trying to shape them into perfect rings, as the dough is quite wet.

CHEESECAKE BROWNIES WITH RASPBERRIES

This has got to be my most requested, most complimented recipe. I've made these brownies all over the world to nothing but rave reviews. The recipe is an adapted version of a brownie from a *delicious* magazine years ago. They are easy to make, yet taste like absolute heaven. You can even use a whisk if you don't have electric beaters; just make sure the cream cheese is at room temperature before you begin. Good-quality dark chocolate is also important. Using one containing at least 80% cocoa solids will create the most lush flavour, with plenty of sweetness coming from the brownie and cheesecake layers.

——————— Makes about 20 small brownies • gluten free, leftovers friendly ———————

INGREDIENTS:

250 g (9 oz) good-quality dark chocolate (80% cocoa)

200 g (7 oz) butter, softened

5 eggs

400 g (14 oz/1¾ cups) caster (superfine) sugar

pinch of sea salt

2 tsp natural vanilla extract

75 g (2¾ oz/½ cup) plain (all-purpose) flour (or gluten-free flour)

350 g (12½ oz) cream cheese, softened

185 g (6½ oz/1½ cups) fresh or frozen raspberries

METHOD:

Preheat the oven to 170°C (340°F). Line a medium-sized brownie tray with baking paper.

In a microwave on low, or in a carefully watched saucepan, melt the chocolate and butter together until smooth and combined. Set aside to cool slightly.

Beat or whisk three of the eggs and 285 g (10 oz/1¼ cups) of the caster sugar until thick and pale—about 2 minutes. Add the sea salt and 1 teaspoon of the vanilla and beat to combine. Pour in the melted chocolate mixture and beat until just combined. Spoon in the flour and stir with a wooden spoon until just mixed in.

Meanwhile, beat the remaining sugar, vanilla, eggs and cream cheese until smooth and silky; if you're whisking, don't fret if there are a few lumps.

Pour the chocolate mixture evenly into the lined tray, reserving a few tablespoons. Spoon the cream cheese mixture in blobs over the top of the batter and gently spread it out as much as you can. Spoon the remaining chocolate mixture over the top. Use a butter knife to swirl the top layer to create a nice pattern with the two batters. Evenly distribute the raspberries on top.

Bake for 30–40 minutes, or until just cooked in the centre. Allow the brownies to cool completely before slicing—or just eat them warm from the tin with a spoon!

BANANA, TAHINI AND DATE CAKE WITH RICOTTA FILLING

Inspired by the famed chef Yotam Ottolenghi, this cake is an unusual but serious crowd-pleaser. The flavour combination of sweet dates, creamy ricotta and banana, offset by a lovely hum of tahini, make this cake wonderfully special. The base is incredibly moist, and the ricotta layer provides a nice surprise when you cut into it. I love the addition of cream cheese icing, with caramelised banana and toasted seeds. However, this cake is also lovely nude if you want to keep things simple. A couple of easy substitutions will make the cake batter vegan, and you can omit the ricotta layer and icing, or use vegan cream cheese if available.

———————————— Makes one 22 cm (8¾ inch) cake • vegan option, leftovers friendly ————————————

INGREDIENTS:

3 small bananas (or 2 large)

3 tbsp sesame seeds, toasted

3 tbsp tahini

80 ml (2½ fl oz/⅓ cup) buttermilk (see note) or nut milk

80 g (2¾ oz/½ cup) chopped pitted dates

125 ml (4 fl oz/½ cup) vegetable oil

2 large eggs, or an extra 80 ml (2½ fl oz/⅓ cup) nut milk

170 g (6 oz/¾ cup) caster (superfine) sugar

260 g (9 oz/1¾ cups) self-raising flour

Ricotta Filling

200 g (7 oz) ricotta

1 egg

115 g (4 oz/½ cup) caster (superfine) sugar

1 tsp natural vanilla extract

Icing and Toppings

200 g (7 oz) cream cheese, at room temperature

185 g (6½ oz/1½ cups) icing (confectioners') sugar

1 tsp natural vanilla extract

2 tbsp tahini

2 bananas, each sliced into 3 pieces, diagonally lengthways

20 g (¾ oz) butter

2 tbsp maple syrup (optional)

METHOD:

Preheat the oven to 180°C (350°F). Line a 22 cm (8¾ inch) round cake tin with baking paper.

Mash the bananas in a large mixing bowl using a fork. Add 2 tablespoons of the sesame seeds, the tahini, buttermilk, dates, vegetable oil and eggs. Whisk the mixture well until combined. Add the sugar, flour, and a pinch of salt and stir well until the dry ingredients are completely incorporated.

In a separate bowl, whisk all the ricotta filling ingredients until smooth.

Spoon half the cake batter into the lined cake tin. Use a spoon to create a large, shallow well in the batter, then pour the ricotta mixture into the well. Gently spoon the remaining cake batter over the top, so that it completely covers the ricotta mix.

Bake for 40 minutes, or until a skewer comes out clean. Remove the cake from the tin and allow it to cool completely.

Meanwhile, prepare the icing by beating the cream cheese and icing sugar together until combined—about 1 minute. Add the vanilla and tahini and beat again until thick and smooth. Prepare the banana by heating a large, non-stick frying pan. Add the butter to the pan. Once sizzling hot, add the banana slices. Cook on each side for 1–2 minutes, until brown. Remove from the pan and set aside.

Once the cake is cooled, transfer to a serving plate. Top with the tahini cream cheese icing, spreading the icing to cover the top of the cake. Gently arrange the banana pieces on top in the centre. Sprinkle with the remaining sesame seeds, and drizzle with the maple syrup, if desired.

Notes: You can make buttermilk by mixing 80 ml (2½ fl oz/⅓ cup) cow's milk with 2 teaspoons lemon juice. Allow the mixture to sit for a minute and thicken slightly.

The caramelised bananas can also be prepared using an oven grill on a very high heat. Lay the banana slices on a baking tray and sprinkle with a little caster (superfine) sugar instead of the butter. Grill until the sugar is melting and turning dark brown.

Chapter Four

EAT IT WITH YOUR HANDS

Orleigh Street

ORLEIGH STREET:
EAT IT WITH YOUR HANDS

Picnics are for sharing food in its lowest-fuss form. All the recipes in this chapter transport well, don't require plates or cutlery, and are perfectly delicious lukewarm or even cold. We photographed this picnic with a group of mates in the much-loved Orleigh Park, by the Brisbane River. This park is the site of many a birthday celebration, public holiday or Sunday afternoon gathering, and felt like a must-include location in the book. Issy, Mon, Dan, Ella, Max, Maddie and Jackson joined the feast on this particular occasion.

Chickpea Sandwich Filling

Focaccia Bread Two Ways (Asparagus and Mozzarella Topped; Antipasto Stuffed)

Beetroot and Labneh Savoury Tart

Loaded Baked Brie

Four Easy Dips (Baba Ghanoush; Olive and Mint Tapenade; Kale Pesto;
Creamy Carrot, Cashew and Dill)

Vegan Hummingbird Cake

Browned Butter, Double Choc Chip Bikkies

Layered Caramel and Chocolate Slice

CHICKPEA SANDWICH FILLING

I absolutely love this stuff. It isn't the most visually striking mixture in the world—and it's
pretty basic, really—but I could eat it in a wrap or on a good piece of toasted Turkish bread
just about every day, I think. The creamy avocado that binds it all together has such a lovely,
light consistency, and the crunch from the celery, apple and onion adds an interesting texture.
I like it a lot with dill, but you could use different herbs—basil, parsley or coriander (cilantro)
would all be nice. For the texture, it's really important to dice the vegies as finely as you can.
Alternatively, you could use a food processor on pulse mode.

Makes enough for about 8 sandwiches • vegan, gluten free, leftovers friendly

INGREDIENTS:

3 celery stalks, finely diced

½ red onion, finely diced

1 small green apple, finely diced

1 large handful finely chopped herbs
(I usually use dill and parsley)

4 tbsp finely diced pickled cucumbers

2 × 400 g (14 oz) tins chickpeas,
drained

2 ripe avocados

1 tbsp lemon juice

2 tsp curry powder

2 tbsp olive oil

METHOD:

Combine the celery, onion, apple, herbs and pickled cucumbers in a large bowl.

In a smaller bowl using a fork, or in a food processor on the pulse setting, mash the
chickpeas to crush them, without blending to a paste. Add the crushed chickpeas to
the celery mixture.

Blend or mash the avocado with the lemon juice, curry powder and olive oil until
smooth. Add to the celery mixture and stir until combined, then season well with
salt and pepper to taste.

The mixture will keep covered in the fridge for up to 2 days.

FOCACCIA BREAD TWO WAYS

So delicious and so economical, focaccia bread is perfect for a picnic or easy lunch. It's really versatile, too, in terms of the different ingredients you can add. Here, I've done it two ways: one baked simply, then topped with ribbons of asparagus, mozzarella, mint and a sprinkling of pine nuts, almost like a very thick crusted pizza; the other stuffed full of caramelised onion, olives, marinated artichokes, sun-dried tomatoes and garlic. These are just two suggestions though, as this recipe is incredibly flexible. Add whatever you like to your dough and mix it in, or cook it on top. Roasted potato with rosemary is lovely, as is a pesto pumpkin (winter squash) stuffing. You can also bake the focaccia as is, then slice it in half lengthways, stuff it with your favourite roast vegies and eat it as a toasted sandwich.

Makes 2 trays of focaccia • vegan option, leftovers friendly

FOCACCIA BREAD TWO WAYS

INGREDIENTS:

Focaccia Base

435 ml (15 fl oz/1¾ cups) warm water

2 tsp active dried yeast (1 × 7 g sachet)

1 tbsp sugar

675 g (1½ lb/4½ cups) plain (all-purpose) flour, plus extra for dusting

1 tbsp salt, plus coarse sea salt and pepper, for sprinkling

125 ml (4 fl oz/½ cup) olive oil, plus extra for drizzling

1 small handful rosemary leaves

Asparagus and Mozzarella Topped

2 bunches asparagus, shaved using a vegetable peeler

200 g (7 oz) mozzarella or bocconcini, roughly sliced

1 large handful mint, chopped

zest and juice of 1 lemon

1 tbsp salt

4 tbsp pine nuts

Antipasto Stuffed

1 tbsp olive oil

1 red onion, thinly sliced

4 garlic cloves, sliced

110 g (4 oz/½ cup) roughly chopped marinated artichoke hearts

155 g (5½ oz/1 cup) pitted olives, roughly chopped

160 g (5½ oz/1 cup) roughly chopped sun-dried tomatoes

1 large handful herbs, such as basil, rosemary, oregano, parsley and/or thyme, chopped

METHOD FOR PLAIN FOCACCIA:

In a small bowl, combine the warm water, yeast and sugar. Leave the bowl in a warm place for about 10 minutes, until the mixture is bubbling.

Add the flour, salt and olive oil. Stir with a fork until the mixture comes together as a dough. Dump onto a floured surface and knead for about 5–8 minutes, until soft and elastic. Transfer to a clean bowl and drizzle on some more olive oil. Cover with a clean cloth and leave in a warm place for 30 minutes, or until doubled in size; the rising time will depend on the level of heat and humidity.

Pour a large glug of olive oil onto two baking trays and add the risen dough. Stretch the dough to fit the trays, add a sprinkling of salt, and scatter the rosemary over the top. Leave to rise again for another 20 minutes or so.

While the dough is rising, preheat the oven to 200°C (400°F). Before baking, press finger holes all through the dough, pushing the rosemary in.

Bake for about 25 minutes, or until golden and cooked through.

METHOD FOR ASPARAGUS AND MOZZARELLA TOPPED:

Make the plain dough as directed above and shape into two focaccias. After the dough has risen a second time, bake the focaccias for 15 minutes.

While the focaccias are in the oven, combine all the topping ingredients in a bowl, along with cracked pepper to taste.

After 15 minutes of baking, or when the bread is beginning to colour, remove the focaccias from the oven and scatter the topping over them, pressing it in slightly with your hands.

Bake for a further 10 minutes, or until the cheese is golden and melted and the bread is cooked through.

METHOD FOR ANTIPASTO STUFFED:

Make the plain focaccia dough, kneading it together as directed and leaving it in the bowl for its first rising.

While you're waiting for the dough to rise, heat a large frying pan with the olive oil. Add the onion and cook over medium heat for 5–10 minutes, or until caramelised and translucent. Add all the remaining ingredients to the pan, along with a sprinkling of salt and cracked pepper. Cook for a couple of minutes, then set the mixture aside.

Once the dough has doubled in size, use your hands to knock out the air. Pour the antipasto mixture into the bowl. Use your hands to massage the mixture so the antipasto spreads throughout the dough evenly.

Shape into two focaccias, leave to rise a second time, then bake as directed in the plain focaccia recipe.

BEETROOT AND LABNEH SAVOURY TART

A beautiful tart is the perfect picnic centrepiece. Roasting the beetroot and finishing it with honey creates the most lovely sweetness, which is offset by the slight sourness of the labneh. This tart is super flexible. Soft feta or goat's cheese would be equally delicious if you can't get your hands on labneh; you could also try other topping combinations, such as roasted tomatoes, pumpkin (winter squash) and pine nuts; garlic and thyme mushrooms with feta; or simply caramelised herby onions with cheddar.

Nailing the pastry is the trick. Make sure the butter is super cold, and leave in some slightly bigger chunks of butter for a lovely, flaky pastry. When handling the pastry, only use your fingertips (because your hands are very warm), and avoid touching the pastry as much as possible. Also, make sure it's seasoned well. Of course, you can also use pre-made pastry, which is a great quick option and quite often vegan too.

--- Makes 1 tart • leftovers friendly, freezer friendly ---

INGREDIENTS:

3 medium beetroot, peeled and cut into thin wedges

2 tbsp olive oil

½ tsp salt

1 tbsp honey

200 g (7 oz) ricotta

zest of ½ lemon

1 egg

100 g (3½ oz) labneh

25 g (1 oz/¼ cup) walnuts, roughly chopped

1 tbsp rosemary leaves

Pastry

225 g (8 oz/1½ cups) plain (all-purpose) flour, plus extra for dusting

75 g (2¾ oz) chilled butter, chopped

1 tsp salt

1 egg yolk

3 tbsp iced water

METHOD:

Preheat the oven to 200°C (400°F). Arrange the beetroot slices on a baking tray and drizzle half the olive oil over the top. Sprinkle with the salt and bake for 30–40 minutes, or until the beetroot slices are beginning to soften and crisp up. Remove from the oven and drizzle with the honey. Set aside and keep the oven warm.

While the beetroot is roasting, make a start on the pastry. Combine the flour, butter and salt with your fingertips until small crumbs form. Add the egg yolk and iced water and bring the dough together with your hands into one ball. Place in a bowl and cover with a clean cloth. Chill for at least 15 minutes.

While the pastry is resting, mix the ricotta, lemon zest, egg and a generous sprinkling of salt and pepper together in a small bowl.

Line a round baking tray with baking paper. On a well-floured surface, roll out the pastry dough into a large, thin circle, no more than 5 mm (¼ inch) thick. Transfer carefully to the lined baking tray; don't worry if it hangs over the sides of the tray for now.

Pour the ricotta mixture into the centre of the pastry and spread evenly to about 3 cm (1¼ inches) from the edge. Arrange the beetroot slices on top, then add the labneh, swirling it or placing blobs evenly around. Scatter the walnuts and rosemary over the top. Sprinkle with salt and pepper and drizzle with the remaining olive oil.

Fold the rim of the dough up and over the edge of the filling, then work around the whole tart, crimping the edges up and over.

Bake the tart for 20–30 minutes, or until the pastry is golden brown and cooked on the bottom. Serve hot or at room temperature.

LOADED BAKED BRIE

Baked brie is a massive crowd-pleaser. It's absolutely beautiful and very easy to create.
Camembert works just as well too, but it's essential that you use a whole wheel of cheese,
rather than a wedge, or you'll have a melted explosion on your hands.

You can top these babies with just about anything, depending on your taste, and what you have
available. I think the key is to have plenty of sweetness on top (chutney, cranberry sauce, honey,
jam or even just brown sugar), along with some texture (nuts, seeds) and extra flavour (balsamic
vinegar, herbs, pesto). Some of my favourite toppings are: walnuts, pesto, chilli jam or fresh chilli,
pine nuts, sliced and roasted mushrooms or capsicum (bell pepper), and herbs of any kind.

Another big bonus is that you can assemble everything ahead of time, then simply bake
the cheese wheels when you're ready to eat.

Makes 2 wheels; serves 10 as a starter

INGREDIENTS:

1 tbsp olive oil, plus extra for drizzling

1 tbsp butter

1 large red onion, sliced

2 tbsp brown sugar

3 tbsp balsamic vinegar, plus extra
for drizzling

4 tbsp pepitas (pumpkin seeds)

1 tbsp honey

2 tsp smoked paprika

2–3 tbsp cranberry sauce

2 wheels of brie, each weighing about
200–250 g (7–9 oz)

1 handful thyme leaves

1 handful rosemary leaves

toasted baguette slices, bread or
crackers, to serve

METHOD:

Preheat the oven to 180°C (350°F).

In a frying pan, heat the olive oil and butter. Add the onion and cook over medium
heat for about 10 minutes, stirring often. Once the onion has started caramelising,
add the sugar, 2 tablespoons of the balsamic vinegar, and salt and pepper to taste.
Cook for a further 5–10 minutes, stirring often. If the onion seems too sticky, add
another splash of vinegar. Transfer to a bowl.

Add the pepitas to the same pan with another drizzle of olive oil. Cook over low
heat until the seeds begin to pop. Add the honey, paprika and a good pinch of salt.
Cook for another 1–2 minutes, then set aside.

To assemble, place the wheels of cheese on a baking tray lined with baking paper.
Spread the cranberry sauce over each one, then top with the balsamic onion. Divide
the herbs over each wheel, reserving a few sprigs for garnishing. Add the honeyed
pumpkin seeds. Finish by drizzling a little more olive oil and vinegar over the top.

Bake for about 15 minutes, or until the toppings are sizzling hot and the inside of
the cheese is melted (the wheels will have slumped, as they'll be runny inside).

Garnish with the reserved herbs and serve immediately, with your carb of choice.

FOUR EASY DIPS

I love making big bowls of dips to share with mates, served up with lots of good bread or homemade focaccia and vegie sticks. These four vegan dips are so easy and versatile, and show how simple it is to turn some vegies, oils and nuts into something wonderful for a picnic or party spread. These four vegan dips are all vegetable based, but think of incorporating other pantry staples such as beans, pulses and herbs, and the options for making a whole range of other delicious dips are just about endless. My philosophy on a good dip is that pre-roasting any solid vegetable is essential for good flavour, that roasted garlic makes just about any dip better, and that a decent seasoning with salt is crucial.

You'll need a food processor to make these dips.

—— Each dip makes 1 small bowl, serving about 6 • vegan, gluten free, leftovers friendly, freezer friendly ——

BABA GHANOUSH

INGREDIENTS:

1 large eggplant (aubergine)

1 tbsp tahini

1 tbsp lemon juice

1 tsp ground cumin

3 tbsp olive oil

1 garlic clove, peeled

salt and pepper, to taste

METHOD:

Preheat the oven to 200°C (400°F). Roast the eggplant whole on a baking tray for about 1 hour, or until the skin is black and the inside is soft. Remove from the oven and set aside to cool.

Scrape out the eggplant flesh, discarding the burnt skin, and blend in a food processor with all the remaining ingredients until well mixed. Season to taste.

Transfer to a bowl and serve.

OLIVE AND MINT TAPENADE

INGREDIENTS:

200 g (7 oz) pitted olives

1 handful mint leaves

60 g (2 oz/½ cup) walnuts, toasted

½ fresh chilli, seeds removed

juice of ½ lemon

125 ml (4 fl oz/½ cup) olive oil

½ tsp salt

METHOD:

Blend all the ingredients in a food processor on pulse mode to form a thick, chunky dip.

Season to taste. Transfer to a bowl and serve.

KALE PESTO

INGREDIENTS:

2 large handfuls chopped kale

1 bunch basil, leaves picked

2 garlic cloves, peeled

80 g (2¾ oz/½ cup) pine nuts, toasted

1 tbsp lemon juice

250 ml (8½ fl oz/1 cup) good olive oil

2 tsp salt

cracked black pepper, to taste

METHOD:

Blend all the ingredients in a food processor until smooth.

Taste the pesto and adjust the seasoning to your liking.

Transfer to a bowl and serve.

CREAMY CARROT, CASHEW AND DILL

INGREDIENTS:

2 large carrots, cut into 1 cm (½ inch) chunks

4 garlic cloves, skin on

125 ml (4 fl oz/½ cup) olive oil

3 tbsp nutritional yeast

80 g (2¾ oz/½ cup) raw cashew nuts

½ bunch dill, roughly chopped

½ tsp salt

METHOD:

Preheat the oven to 180°C (350°F). Arrange the carrots and garlic cloves in a small baking dish. Pour the olive oil over and sprinkle with salt.

Bake for 30 minutes, or until the carrot is browning and the garlic is a deep golden colour and soft in the middle.

Remove from the oven and transfer to a blender. Add the remaining ingredients and blend until smooth.

Check the seasoning and adjust to your taste. Transfer to a bowl and serve.

VEGAN HUMMINGBIRD CAKE

Hummingbird cake is one of my all-time favourites. Packed with interesting flavours and textures, it's something a little different, and is perfect as a special occasion treat. It's also light enough to be enjoyed for morning or afternoon tea. I love this vegan version, in which vegetable oil is substituted for the butter, giving the cake its wonderful moistness. You can find vegan cream cheese at most shops that offer a good vegan selection. Alternatively, if you eat animal products, you can use regular cream cheese.

Makes one 24 cm (9½ inch) cake • vegan, leftovers friendly

VEGAN HUMMINGBIRD CAKE

INGREDIENTS:

3 large, overripe bananas, mashed

200 g (7 oz/¾ cup) crushed tinned pineapple, plus 125 ml (4 fl oz/½ cup) of the pineapple juice

250 ml (8½ fl oz/1 cup) vegetable oil

345 g (12 oz/1½ cups) caster (superfine) sugar

125 ml (4 fl oz/½ cup) unsweetened apple sauce

3 tbsp soy milk

2 tsp natural vanilla extract

1 tsp apple cider vinegar

450 g (1 lb/3 cups) plain (all-purpose) flour

1 tsp bicarbonate of soda (baking soda)

1½ tsp baking powder

1 tsp ground cinnamon

½ tsp salt

55 g (2 oz/1 cup) flaked coconut

90 g (3 oz/¾ cup) chopped pecans

Maple Pecans

125 g (4½ oz/1 cup) chopped pecans

80 ml (2½ fl oz/⅓ cup) maple syrup

Icing

250 g (9 oz) vegan cream cheese, softened

125 g (4½ oz) vegan margarine, softened

1 tsp natural vanilla extract

310 g (11 oz/2½ cups) icing (confectioners') sugar

METHOD:

Preheat the oven to 180°C (350°F). Line a 24 cm (9½ inch) round cake tin with baking paper.

In a large bowl, mash the bananas, pineapple and pineapple juice together using a fork. Add the vegetable oil, sugar, apple sauce, soy milk, vanilla and vinegar. Whisk well to combine.

In a separate bowl, mix together the flour, bicarbonate of soda, baking powder, cinnamon and salt.

Add the flour mixture to the batter and whisk until just combined; make sure you don't overmix, so the mixture doesn't become tough. Add the coconut and pecans and gently stir them through. Pour the mixture into the lined cake tin.

Bake for about 35–40 minutes, or until golden. The top of the cake should spring back slightly when touched, and a knife should come out almost clean. Remove from the oven and allow the cake to cool completely.

Turn the oven down to 160°C (320°F) for the maple pecans. Spread the pecans on a large baking tray lined with baking paper. Drizzle the maple syrup evenly over the nuts. Bake for 20 minutes, or until the maple syrup has been boiling and bubbling for about 10 minutes. Remove from the oven and leave to cool completely.

To make the icing, place the cream cheese and margarine in a mixing bowl and blend together using electric beaters. Add the vanilla and beat in well. Add the icing sugar in three batches, beating well in between. Set aside at room temperature until you're ready to ice the cake.

Once the cake and maple pecans are both completely cooled, spread the icing evenly over the top of the cake. Use a mallet or knife to crush the nuts into shards or big chunks (or put them in a plastic bag, then wrap in a cloth, and smash with a mallet or rolling pin). Sprinkle the nuts over the cake.

Notes: I store overripe bananas in the freezer, where they keep for ages and retain the delicious flavour that only comes from almost-too-mushy bananas. Simply defrost and use whenever the urge to bake strikes.

For super-silky cream cheese icing, ensure both the margarine and cream cheese are softened to room temperature before using.

BROWNED BUTTER, DOUBLE CHOC CHIP BIKKIES

Inspired by traditional Italian-style almond biscuits and born from a desire not to waste egg whites at a café I was working at, these bikkies were a bit of a fluke creation. The expression 'perfect chocolate chip cookie' gets thrown around a lot these days, and I know everyone likes their cookies a little bit differently, but look... I reckon these are pretty close. A slight crunch, a bit of bend, a real chew and a beautiful caramel flavour from the browned butter and sugar—they're definitely *my* perfect cookies, that much I can say.

I like my chocolate chip bikkies seriously chocolatey: as in a one-to-one ratio of chocolate to dough. If this isn't your style, feel free to use less chocolate. I also like to use a mixture of milk, dark and white chocolate chips, but, again, it's up to you. Beauty is in the mouth of the beholder.

——————— Makes 15 big bikkies or 24 smaller ones • gluten-free option, leftovers friendly, freezer friendly ———————

INGREDIENTS:

100 g (3½ oz) butter

230 g (8 oz/1 cup) brown sugar

2 egg whites, whisked

1 tsp natural vanilla extract

125 g (4½ oz/1¼ cups) almond meal

75 g (2¾ oz/½ cup) self-raising flour (or use gluten-free)

250 g (9 oz/1½ cups) mixed chocolate chips

METHOD:

Melt the butter in a small saucepan over medium heat. When the butter is almost coming to the boil, reduce the heat and cook slowly, stirring often, until it is beginning to brown and smells very nutty; this should take about 5 minutes.

Pour the browned butter into a large mixing bowl and add the sugar. Mix well to combine and let the mixture cool for 5–10 minutes.

Add the whisked egg whites and vanilla and whisk well. Add the almond meal and flour and stir together with a wooden spoon. The mixture might seem slightly wetter than other biscuit doughs you've made, but don't stress.

Add the chocolate and fold until combined. Cover the bowl and refrigerate for at least 1–2 hours, or up to 2 days. This ensures the bikkies hold their shape when baked.

Around 20 minutes before you're ready to bake, preheat the oven to 180°C (350°F), and line a large biscuit tray with baking paper.

Roll the dough into 15 balls of equal size and arrange evenly around your baking tray. Press each ball down slightly with your fingers.

Bake for 10–12 minutes, or until the bikkies are beginning to turn golden. Be careful not to overcook them, unless you like them super crunchy. When the bottoms are golden and the tops are just the slightest shade darker, they're done. They'll feel super soft to touch when straight out of the oven, but will harden considerably as they cool.

Best eaten with a glass of milk, many would say.

LAYERED CARAMEL AND CHOCOLATE SLICE

This slice is so deliciously chewy, nutty, caramelly, chocolatey and yet somehow pretty healthy—
and vegan! It can easily be tweaked to your taste. I often change the middle layer into a
chocolate fudge by adding 3 tablespoons of cocoa powder, and I've been known to replace
the peanuts with frozen raspberries. You could also try replacing the roasted peanuts with other
nuts or seeds, or omit them altogether.

—————— Makes about 16 pieces • vegan, gluten-free option, leftovers friendly, freezer friendly ——————

INGREDIENTS:

Base

180 g (6½ oz/1 cup) soft pitted dates
(soak them in boiling water for
5 minutes if they aren't soft)

60 g (2 oz/¾ cup) desiccated coconut

80 g (2¾ oz/½ cup) roasted almonds

55 g (2 oz/½ cup) LSA (linseed,
sunflower and almond meal), or plain
almond meal

1 tbsp good-quality cocoa powder

1 tbsp peanut butter

¼ tsp salt

'Caramel'

3 tbsp peanut butter

2 tbsp maple syrup

180 g (6½ oz/1 cup) soft pitted dates

3 tbsp nut milk of choice

pinch of salt

160 g (5½ oz/1 cup) roasted unsalted
peanuts

Chocolate

150 g (5½ oz) dark chocolate
(85% cocoa)

2 tbsp nut milk of choice

sea salt, for sprinkling

METHOD:

Whiz all the base ingredients in a food processor for 1–2 minutes, or until combined
and sticky. Press into a 20 cm (8 inch) baking tray lined with baking paper.

To make the caramel, whiz the peanut butter, maple syrup, dates, nut milk and salt
together for about 1 minute, or until super silky. Stir the roasted nuts through, then
pour over the base and spread evenly.

For the chocolate layer, melt the chocolate and nut milk together in a microwave, or
gently in a saucepan over the stove. Pour the mixture over the nutty caramel, then
sprinkle sea salt over the top.

Transfer the slice to the freezer to set for at least 30 minutes; it needs to be
completely firm for slicing.

Store in the fridge if you don't mind it fudgy, or in the freezer if you prefer it solid.

Note: This recipe requires a food processor or good-quality blender.

Chapter Five

A MEXICAN—INSPIRED FEAST

MACARTNEY STREET:
A MEXICAN-INSPIRED FEAST

Mexican is one of my favourite cuisines to cook for a crowd. I'm constantly inspired by the seemingly endless flavour possibilities offered by ingredients such as lime, coriander, cumin and paprika. This feast is so flavourful and fresh, and many of these dishes also make perfect weeknight meals on their own. We enjoyed this feast in the garden of a great old sharehouse in Brisbane's Paddington, with Annie, Claudia and Erin.

Empanadas with Barbecue Shredded Jackfruit and Vegan Chipotle Mayo

Jalapeño Cornbread

Black Bean and Quinoa Chilli

Roasted Sweet Potato and Bean Enchiladas with Chimichurri Sauce

Charred Pineapple Salsa

Barbecue Corn on the Cob with all the Trimmings

EMPANADAS WITH BARBECUE SHREDDED JACKFRUIT AND VEGAN CHIPOTLE MAYO

If you've never used jackfruit as a meat replacement, you're seriously missing out. The tinned stuff is the way to go, and is most readily available from Asian food stores; just be sure to buy it in brine, not syrup. You'd be wise to double the quantity of jackfruit filling below and save some to use in sandwiches, burgers, tacos or on rice, as it is incredibly delicious and super versatile. These empanadas are great hot, but they also work at room temperature. The vegan chipotle mayo is a lovely accompaniment, but you can save yourself some labour and use ready-made mayo swirled with chipotle sauce.

Makes 12 empanadas • vegan, leftovers friendly, freezer friendly

INGREDIENTS:

2 tbsp olive oil

1 red onion, very thinly sliced

1 red capsicum (bell pepper), cut into long thin strips

3 garlic cloves, crushed

1 tsp ground cumin

1 tsp ground coriander

1 tsp smoked paprika

450 g (1 lb) tin jackfruit in brine, drained and chopped

3 tbsp barbecue sauce

1 tbsp whiskey or bourbon (optional)

3 sheets shortcrust pastry

500 ml (17 fl oz/2 cups) vegetable or canola oil

Vegan Chipotle Mayo

3 tbsp soy milk

1 tsp lemon juice

125 ml (4 fl oz/½ cup) vegetable oil

½ tsp dijon mustard or mustard powder

2 tsp chipotle chillies in adobo sauce

METHOD:

Heat the olive oil in a large, heavy-based frying pan over high heat. Add the onion and capsicum and cook for 5 minutes, stirring every 1–2 minutes, allowing the vegetables to sear and burn slightly on the edges.

Add the garlic, spices and chopped jackfruit. Stir for a couple of minutes to combine well.

Stir in the barbecue sauce and alcohol, if using. Sprinkle with salt and pepper, add a splash of water, then reduce the heat and cook for about 10–15 minutes, stirring occasionally. Turn the heat off and allow the mixture to cool well.

Meanwhile, make the mayo. Combine the soy milk and lemon juice in a blender (or emulsify with a stick blender in a bowl) for about 20 seconds. While blending, slowly add in the vegetable oil until the oil is emulsified and the mixture thickens. Add the mustard and a pinch of salt and continue to blend. Taste and adjust the seasoning to your liking. Swirl the chipotles and their sauce in gently so the mixture is not fully combined. Set aside.

Cut each sheet of pastry into four large rounds using a cookie cutter, individual tart tin or sharp-edged bowl.

Place 1 heaped tablespoon of the jackfruit mixture in the centre of each pastry round, fold over into a half-moon and seal the edges with your fingers.

Heat the vegetable oil in a large frying pan until sizzling hot. Test the oil is hot enough by placing a small piece of leftover pastry in it. If the pastry sizzles, the oil is ready.

Fry the empanadas, six at a time, for a minute or so on each side. Turn with tongs and repeat on the other side.

Serve the empanadas with the chipotle mayo on the side.

JALAPEÑO CORNBREAD

Everyone goes wild for this one. Perfect on its own with some butter, and even better served alongside a bowl of Mexican chilli con/sin carne, this delicious cornbread is slightly spiced and perfectly crumbly. Plus it's surprisingly easy to prepare, using minimal equipment. Here I've made loaves, but the same recipe would work in muffin tins. Truly incredible fresh out of the oven, the cornbread is also freezable and reheatable.

Makes 2 loaves • vegan option, gluten-free option, leftovers friendly, freezer friendly

INGREDIENTS:

100 g (3½ oz) butter (or vegan margarine), melted

3 tbsp olive oil

3 eggs, or 3 tbsp non-dairy milk

310 ml (10½ fl oz/1¼ cups) buttermilk (or milk plus 2 tsp lemon juice); use non-dairy milk if vegan

3 corn cobs, kernels stripped, or 2 × 400 g (14 oz) tins corn kernels

300 g (10½ oz/2 cups) self-raising flour (or gluten-free flour)

225 g (8 oz/1½ cups) instant polenta or cornmeal

3 tbsp white or caster (superfine) sugar

2 tsp salt

2 tbsp chopped jalapeño chillies

3 tbsp chopped coriander (cilantro); optional, but delicious

grated cheddar cheese (or nutritional yeast), for sprinkling

sunflower seeds or pepitas (pumpkin seeds), for sprinkling (optional)

METHOD:

Preheat the oven to 200°C (400°F). Line two loaf (bar) tins with baking paper.

Place the butter, olive oil, eggs and buttermilk in a large bowl and whisk together. Add the corn kernels, flour, polenta, sugar, salt, chillies and coriander, if using. Stir gently until just combined.

Pour the mixture into the lined loaf tins. Sprinkle each with cheese, and some seeds, if using. Bake for about 30 minutes, or until the loaves are golden and a knife comes out clean.

Let the loaves cool on a rack before slicing.

BLACK BEAN AND QUINOA CHILLI

Vegie chilli has been a staple in my diet since I stopped buying meat, and once I discovered how amazing the addition of quinoa is in creating a hearty 'meat-like' texture, I haven't gone back. If you'd prefer to use TVP (textured vegetable protein) or vegan mince, they would both be equally delicious. You could add a tin of corn at the end, some kidney beans, spinach, roasted sweet potato, any vegies that need using up—anything you please. As long as everything gets at least a good half an hour to bubble away, you can't really go wrong.

I love this chilli bean dish on its own with sour cream or guacamole, and corn chips for dunking, but it's also great in burritos, enchiladas or atop nachos, too.

Serves 4–6 • vegan, gluten free, leftovers friendly, freezer friendly

INGREDIENTS:

2 tbsp olive oil

2 brown onions, diced

2 zucchini (courgettes), diced

1 small capsicum (bell pepper), diced

4 garlic cloves, crushed

2 tsp ground cumin

2 tsp ground coriander

2 tsp paprika

½ tsp chilli powder, or to taste

2 tsp dried oregano

3 × 400 g (14 oz) tins black beans, drained

500 ml (17 fl oz/2 cups) vegetable stock

100 g (3½ oz/½ cup) uncooked quinoa

2 × 400 g (14 oz) tins chopped tomatoes

½ bunch coriander (cilantro), chopped

hot chilli sauce, to taste (optional)

METHOD:

Heat the olive oil in a large, heavy-based pot over medium heat. Add the onions and cook for 10 minutes, stirring every minute or so until they're golden brown.

Add the zucchini, capsicum (and any other vegies you're using), garlic and spices and cook for a further 10 minutes. It's important not to stir too much—only when the vegies on the bottom are browning.

Stir the beans through. Add the stock, quinoa and tomatoes and bring to the boil. Reduce the heat to low and simmer for at least 30 minutes, stirring occasionally to prevent the mixture sticking to the pot.

To finish, turn off the heat and stir the fresh coriander through, plus lots of pepper and salt to taste—and a splash of chilli sauce if you'd like a bit of heat.

Note: This recipe uses tinned black beans, but I usually prepare my own. Cooking 220 g (8 oz/1 cup) dried beans until tender in 750 ml–1 litre (25½–34 fl oz/3–4 cups) vegetable stock will yield a similar quantity.

ROASTED SWEET POTATO AND BEAN ENCHILADAS WITH CHIMICHURRI SAUCE

These enchiladas have a bit of a reputation with my parents, who would request I drop off a tray whenever I was cooking some up. Enchiladas go a long way as part of a feast, but are beautiful as a meal on their own, too, paired with guacamole or a salsa. You can replace the sweet potato with other vegies if you prefer. I usually add some chopped roasted capsicum (bell pepper), or any other vegies that need using up.

If you eat cheese, feta is a lovely addition to the filling.

Makes 14–16 enchiladas in 2 trays • vegan, gluten-free option, leftovers friendly, freezer friendly

ROASTED SWEET POTATO AND BEAN ENCHILADAS WITH CHIMICHURRI SAUCE

INGREDIENTS:

750 g (1 lb 11 oz) sweet potatoes, cut into 1 cm (½ inch) chunks

3 tbsp olive oil

1 large brown onion, diced

3 garlic cloves, crushed

2 tsp salt

1 tbsp ground cumin

1 tbsp ground coriander

1 tbsp smoked paprika

2 tsp dried oregano

2 × 400 g (14 oz) tins chopped tomatoes

2 × 400 g (14 oz) tins kidney beans, drained

14–16 wheat or corn tortillas

70 g (2 oz/½ cup) grated vegan or non-vegan cheese (optional)

Enchilada Sauce

1 tbsp olive oil

2 garlic cloves, crushed

1 tsp salt

2 tsp ground cumin

1 tsp ground coriander

700 g (1 lb 9 oz) jar tomato passata (puréed tomatoes)

Chimichurri Sauce

1 bunch parsley, roughly chopped

1 bunch coriander (cilantro), roughly chopped

2 garlic cloves, peeled

juice of 1 lemon

125 ml (4 fl oz/½ cup) olive oil

1½ tsp white wine vinegar

½ tsp salt

1 tbsp chilli sauce, or ½ chopped fresh chilli, or a pinch of chilli flakes (optional)

METHOD:

Preheat the oven to 200°C (400°F). Spread the sweet potato chunks on a baking tray, then drizzle with 1 tablespoon of the olive oil and sprinkle with salt and pepper. Bake for about 30 minutes, or until soft and browned.

Meanwhile, heat the remaining olive oil in a large saucepan. Add the onion and cook for 5 minutes over medium heat, stirring often, until the onion is golden and softened. Add the garlic, salt and spices and cook for a further few minutes.

Stir in the tomatoes, beans and 3 tablespoons water. Bring to the boil, then reduce the heat and allow the mixture to bubble away for 15–20 minutes. When the sweet potato has finished roasting, stir it all in until combined.

To make the enchilada sauce, heat the olive oil in another saucepan and add the garlic, salt and spices. Cook over low heat for 1–2 minutes. Stir in the passata until well combined, then let the sauce bubble away on low until you need it.

To assemble the enchiladas, place about 3 tablespoons of the bean and sweet potato mixture on a tortilla and roll it into a wrap. Place in a large baking dish. Repeat with all the tortillas until you have two baking dishes filled. Pour the enchilada sauce evenly around each baking dish, top with the grated cheese, if using, then bake for 10–15 minutes, or until the top is browned and the enchilada sauce is bubbling.

Meanwhile, to make the chimichurri sauce, blend all the ingredients together using a food processor, stick blender or mortar and pestle. Taste and add more salt if desired.

When the enchiladas are ready, pour the chimichurri sauce over the top and serve.

Note: If you're using a mortar and pestle to make the chimichurri sauce, you will need to chop the herbs and garlic finely before combining.

CHARRED PINEAPPLE SALSA

Zingy and packed with beautiful flavours, this salsa is the perfect fresh accompaniment to any Mexican meal. It's delicious on tacos and enchiladas, or with some chilli and rice. If you don't have fresh pineapples, you can use tinned—just be sure to drain and pat the slices dry (and keep the juice, as it's delicious added to drinks or smoothies). Grilling the pineapple well, ensuring you get some really nice colour on it, is essential for the smoky flavour of the salsa. The trick is to not turn or move the pineapple too much while it's cooking. Adjust the quantity of chilli to suit your taste, depending on which variety you're using.

Serves 4–6 • vegan, gluten free, leftovers friendly, freezer friendly

INGREDIENTS:

1 large pineapple, or 2 small ones, skin and core removed, flesh cut into 1 cm (½ inch) thick slices

1 chilli, finely chopped

½ bunch mint, finely chopped

1 large bunch coriander (cilantro), finely chopped

3 ripe tomatoes, finely diced

1 small red onion, finely diced

juice of 2 limes

2 tbsp olive oil

METHOD:

Grill the pineapple slices on a hot barbecue, chargrill pan or in a sandwich press until you have some nicely charred grill lines, and significantly less juice is present.

Transfer the grilled pineapple to a chopping board and sprinkle with salt. Allow to cool slightly, then dice into small chunks.

Place the pineapple chunks in a large mixing bowl. Add the remaining ingredients, mixing well with tongs or your hands. Season generously with salt and pepper, and taste to ensure the heat and salt levels are to your liking.

BARBECUE CORN ON THE COB WITH ALL THE TRIMMINGS

I love the combo of creamy, fresh and smoky flavours here. This is such an easy side dish to prepare, but is always such a winner. After all, who doesn't love eating corn on the cob with their hands? I like to cut the cobs into small pieces to enjoy as part of a big shared meal, but you can easily keep them whole. And if you don't have access to a barbecue, just cook them in a frying pan. If you have any leftover cobs, cut off all the kernels and store them in the fridge. They're delicious added to cornbread (see page 123) or a chilli bean dish.

Makes 6 big portions, or 18 small • vegan option, gluten free

INGREDIENTS:

6 corn cobs, husks and silks removed, cut into thirds

2 tbsp olive oil

250 g (9 oz/1 cup) sour cream (or vegan mayonnaise, or cashew cream)

1 tbsp lemon juice

½ tsp salt

2 tsp ground cumin

1 tbsp sweet paprika

1 tsp chilli powder, or ¼ tsp cayenne pepper

50 g (1¾ oz/½ cup) finely grated parmesan (or nutritional yeast)

4 spring onions (scallions), very finely chopped

1 chilli, thinly sliced

½ bunch coriander (cilantro), finely chopped

METHOD:

Drizzle the corn with the olive oil and cook on a hot barbecue grill for 20 minutes, turning every 5 minutes, until the kernels are a bright golden yellow, and slightly blackened in parts.

Meanwhile, in a small bowl, mix together the sour cream, lemon juice and salt.

In another small bowl, combine the cumin, paprika and chilli powder, along with an extra pinch of salt and pepper.

Lay the cooked corn on a platter or serving dish and sprinkle with the spice mix. Move the pieces around to coat well.

Drizzle the sour cream mixture over the corn. Sprinkle the parmesan, spring onions, chilli and coriander over the top and serve.

Chapter Six

A MEDITERRANEAN DINNER PARTY

Locke Street

LOCKE STREET:
A MEDITERRANEAN DINNER PARTY

Everyone needs some classy favourites for a special occasion. The dishes in this chapter are based around simple Mediterranean pantry staples such as polenta, lemons, tomatoes, basil and, of course, olive oil, but elevated to a high level of snazzy deliciousness. Here you'll find some of the more fiddly recipes in the book, perfect for when you have a little time up your sleeve. We shot this chapter in a beautiful home, borrowed from Jackson's family in the Brisbane suburb of New Farm. Emily, Renan, Jackie, Mindy, Sancintya and Jackson joined in for the occasion.

Mushroom and Goat's Cheese Arancini Balls

Blistered Tomato and Olive Bruschetta

Eggplant Parmigiana

Roasted Garlic and Rosemary Polenta Squares

Marinated Zucchini, Asparagus and Haloumi

Roasted Pumpkin with Toasted Crumbs, Maple and Sesame

Stacked Passionfruit and Lemon Pavlova Cake

Lemon and Almond Italian Biscuits

MUSHROOM AND GOAT'S CHEESE ARANCINI BALLS

In my former job as a caterer, I would always be put in charge of the arancini balls, sometimes rolling and stuffing several hundred back-to-back. Tedious work to some, but it was my absolute favourite job—drifting off into my thoughts or getting carried away by the kitchen conversations around me, while methodically working my way through mountains of rice. These arancini balls are a perfect starter or addition to a special meal. The simple flavour combination is delicious, and they're brilliant with a creamy pesto dipping sauce, aioli, or a tomato-based chutney. Crumbing the balls in polenta, rather than breadcrumbs, keeps them gluten-free and holds them together when frying. You can also fry these ahead of time and reheat them in the oven.

Makes about 20 balls • vegan option, gluten free, leftovers friendly, freezer friendly

INGREDIENTS:

225 g (8 oz/1½ cups) polenta

about 1 litre (34 fl oz/4 cups) vegetable or other frying oil

dipping sauce of choice, to serve

Rice

2 tbsp olive oil

450 g (1 lb/2 cups) arborio rice

250 ml (8½ fl oz/1 cup) white wine

1.25 litres (42 fl oz/5 cups) stock

60 g (2 oz/⅔ cup) grated parmesan (or nutritional yeast)

Filling

3 tbsp olive oil

500 g (1 lb 2 oz) mixed mushrooms, chopped into small pieces, 1 cm (½ inch) in size or less

5 garlic cloves, thinly sliced

1 tbsp thyme leaves

1 large handful basil leaves, finely chopped

juice of ½ lemon

125 g (4½ oz) goat's cheese, crumbled (or vegan cheese)

METHOD:

To prepare the rice, heat the olive oil in a large, heavy-based saucepan over medium heat. Add the rice and stir to coat in the oil, cooking for 1–2 minutes. Add half the wine and 250 ml (8½ fl oz/1 cup) of the stock, stirring well. Allow the liquid to absorb, then add the remaining wine and another 250 ml (8½ fl oz/1 cup) stock. Keep adding the stock every couple of minutes until the rice is gluggy and well cooked—the grains should be sticking together. Turn off the heat and season well. Add the parmesan and stir to combine.

Put a lid on the saucepan and allow the rice to steam in the residual heat for about 10 minutes. Transfer the rice to a bowl or container and refrigerate for at least 1–2 hours until cooled completely, or overnight.

Prepare the filling by heating the olive oil in a frying pan over high heat. Once the oil is very hot, add the mushrooms and cook for 5–10 minutes on high heat, only stirring every minute, allowing the mushrooms to become golden. Add the garlic and a sprinkling of salt and pepper and cook for another few minutes. Turn off the heat, add the herbs and lemon juice and mix well to combine. Gently fold in the crumbled cheese.

Place the polenta in a bowl, ready to roll the arancini balls in.

Roll the cooled rice into golf ball-sized balls, or larger if you prefer. Using your thumb, press a cavity into each ball, making it a bowl shape in the palm of your other hand. Spoon about 1 tablespoon of the mushroom mixture into the cavity, then gently reform the ball, sealing the filling inside. Roll each stuffed ball in the polenta to coat.

Heat a medium-sized saucepan and fill with vegetable oil, ensuring the oil is deeper than your arancini balls so you can deep-fry them. Allow the oil to heat over high heat for 5 minutes or so. Test the oil is hot enough by placing one ball in it; it should sizzle. Fry the arancini in batches, keeping the heat on medium and ensuring they have plenty of room in the pan, until the balls are golden and hardened.

Carefully remove the arancini using a slotted spoon and allow to cool on a plate lined with paper towel, to soak up the excess oil.

Serve hot with pesto, aioli or chutney for dipping.

BLISTERED TOMATO AND OLIVE BRUSCHETTA

This bruschetta makes a lovely appetiser or party snack. The trick is using really good tomatoes—fresh, ripe ones that smell like heaven—and to cook them on a high heat to ensure they blister and don't break down and become watery. If you're using cherry tomatoes, either keep them whole or slice them in half, depending on their size. Omit the capers and olives if they're not your cup of tea. Sometimes I also top the bruschetta with some marinated feta, or slices of baked ricotta; a drizzle of pesto or some toasted seeds or pine nuts never go astray, either. The blistered tomato topping will keep for days and is also delicious on its own, and with pasta or soft polenta.

Makes 15–20 pieces • vegan, leftovers friendly

INGREDIENTS:

1 loaf of good-quality ciabatta
or Turkish bread

2 tbsp olive oil

2 garlic cloves, thinly sliced

Blistered Tomato Topping

2 tbsp olive oil, plus extra to serve

1 red onion, thinly sliced

4 ripe tomatoes, thickly sliced

750 g (1 lb 11 oz) mixed heirloom or
cherry tomatoes (a mixture of colours
is lovely)

3 garlic cloves, thinly sliced

1 heaped tbsp capers

40 g (1½ oz/¼ cup) pitted olives,
roughly chopped

2 tsp chopped thyme leaves,
or 1 tsp dried thyme

½ bunch basil, chopped

METHOD:

Preheat the oven to 200°C (400°F).

To make the topping, heat a large frying pan until very hot. Add the olive oil and onion and cook over high heat for a couple of minutes, stirring only every 30 seconds or so to allow the onion to brown quickly.

Add the tomatoes, garlic, capers and olives. Cook over high heat for 5–10 minutes, stirring infrequently, until the tomatoes are blistered. Add the thyme and most of the basil, reserving some basil for garnishing. Season well.

Meanwhile, cut the bread into slices about 1 cm (½ inch) thick. Combine the olive oil and garlic in a small bowl with some salt and pepper. Brush the garlic oil over the bread slices, place on a baking tray and bake until toasted.

Top each piece of garlic toast with a spoonful of tomato topping and garnish with reserved basil. Drizzle each piece with some more olive oil and add any extra toppings you fancy.

EGGPLANT PARMIGIANA

This is one of my all-time favourite ways with eggplant. The beautiful flavours in this dish are created from simple ingredients, cooked low and slow. The parmigiana is perfect with a side of soft polenta, garlic bread, or pasta simply dressed with pesto or olive oil, garlic, and lots of salt and pepper.

Serves 6–8 • vegan option, gluten free, leftovers friendly, freezer friendly

INGREDIENTS:

5 tbsp olive oil

2 onions, thinly sliced

5 garlic cloves, thinly sliced

250 g (9 oz) cherry tomatoes, halved

2 tbsp finely chopped semi-dried tomatoes

40 g (1½ oz/¼ cup) pitted olives, roughly chopped

2 tsp dried basil

3 eggplants (aubergines), cut into 1–2 cm (½–¾ inch) slabs

2 × 400 g (14 oz) tins chopped tomatoes

3 tbsp water (reserved from rinsing out the tomato tins)

3 tbsp red wine

1 handful basil or parsley leaves, plus extra to garnish

200 g (7 oz) fresh mozzarella or bocconcini, sliced (omit for vegan)

25 g (1 oz/¼ cup) grated parmesan, feta or goat's cheese (omit for vegan)

60 g (2 oz/1 cup) panko breadcrumbs

METHOD:

Preheat the oven to 190°C (375°F). Line two baking trays with baking paper.

Add 2 tablespoons of the olive oil and the onions to a saucepan over medium heat. Reduce the heat and slowly cook the onions for 10–15 minutes, stirring often.

Add the garlic, cherry tomatoes, semi-dried tomatoes, olives and dried basil, along with a generous pinch of salt. Increase the heat slightly and cook, stirring often, for another 10 minutes or so.

Meanwhile, lay the eggplant slices on the lined baking trays. Drizzle the remaining 3 tablespoons olive oil over them and sprinkle with salt and pepper. Bake for 25–35 minutes, turning halfway, until the eggplant is soft to touch and lightly golden. (Alternatively, you can cook the eggplant using a benchtop grill or sandwich press. This requires working in smaller batches, but creates beautifully golden, melt-in-your-mouth eggplant.) Set the cooked eggplant aside until ready to assemble.

Once the tomatoes in the pan have broken down and the sauce is smelling amazing, add the tinned tomatoes, water and wine. Bring to the boil, then reduce the heat to low and allow the sauce to bubble away for at least 30 minutes, or up to 2 hours, adding an extra 125 ml (4 fl oz/½ cup) or so of water if it starts becoming too thick. Turn off the heat and add the basil, stirring it through.

Assemble the parmigiana by laying half the eggplant in a large baking dish. Pour half the sauce over the top and sprinkle over about one-third of the cheese. Layer the remaining eggplant slices on top, then the remaining sauce. Sprinkle with salt and pepper, then top with the remaining cheese. Finish by evenly scattering the breadcrumbs over the whole dish.

Bake for 20 minutes, or until the parmigiana is golden and bubbling. Garnish with extra basil and serve.

Note: As the eggplant slices are the bulk of the dish, it is essential to season each slice generously with salt and pepper.

ROASTED GARLIC AND ROSEMARY POLENTA SQUARES

Crispy on the outside and soft and fragrant on the inside, these little polenta bites are heavenly. You can make bigger versions and eat them with eggs for breakfast, or with ratatouille or another stew. I love them like this, as a side in a big feast. They're beautiful with a tomato chutney, pesto or olive tapenade, but wonderful on their own as well.

Makes about 30 polenta squares; serves 10–12 as a side • vegan option, gluten free

INGREDIENTS:

6 garlic cloves, skin on

3 tbsp olive oil, plus extra for pan-frying

750 ml (25½ fl oz/3 cups) vegetable stock

225 g (8 oz/1½ cups) instant polenta

3 tsp sea salt, plus extra to serve

1 small handful rosemary leaves

50 g (1¾ oz/½ cup) finely grated parmesan (or nutritional yeast)

METHOD:

Preheat the oven to 150°C (300°F). Put the garlic and olive oil in a small ramekin (small enough that the cloves are covered in oil) and sprinkle with a pinch of salt. Bake for 20 minutes, or until the cloves are golden and very soft inside, watching closely to ensure the garlic doesn't burn. Remove from the oven and allow the garlic to cool completely. Squeeze the flesh out of the skin and use a fork to mix it into a paste with the remaining garlic-infused oil.

Meanwhile, bring the stock and 500 ml (17 fl oz/2 cups) water to the boil in a large saucepan. Add the polenta and stir for 5–10 minutes, or until thick and smooth.

Turn off the heat. Chop half the rosemary and add it to the polenta with the garlic paste and salt. Stir well to combine. Add more salt and pepper, to taste.

Pour the mixture into a lined 20 cm (8 inch) square baking tin. Refrigerate for 1–2 hours or overnight, until completely set and cold.

Cut the cold polenta into about 30 rectangles or squares.

Heat 1 cm (½ inch) olive oil in a large frying pan over high heat. Test the oil is hot enough by adding a few rosemary leaves; the oil should sizzle. Add all the remaining rosemary and fry for 1–2 minutes, then remove with a slotted spoon and place in a small bowl with a sprinkle of salt.

In the same oil, fry the polenta in batches until each side is golden, then remove from the oil and drain on paper towel or a clean cloth.

Serve the polenta squares warm, sprinkled with the parmesan, fried rosemary and some extra sea salt. I like to serve them on a bed of salad greens.

Note: You can also crisp up the polenta squares in the oven instead of frying them. After cutting the cold polenta into squares or rectangles, arrange the pieces on a lined baking tray, with a little space between each. Drizzle with olive oil and bake for 20 minutes at 200°C (400°F).

MARINATED ZUCCHINI, ASPARAGUS AND HALOUMI

A wonderful addition to a Mediterranean spread, this dish can also be served warm as a simple dinner with some garlic bread. It transports well (think picnic plate), and is beautiful cold as a salad, as the flavours are lovely and fresh. Feel free to replace the sunflower seeds with pine nuts or even walnuts.

Serves 6–8 • vegan option, gluten free

INGREDIENTS:

3 zucchini (courgettes), cut into 5 mm (¼ inch) ribbons

2 bunches asparagus, halved

3 tbsp olive oil, plus extra for pan-frying

½ red onion, very thinly sliced

2 garlic cloves, crushed

zest and juice of 1 small lemon

1 tsp apple cider vinegar

½ tsp chilli flakes

2 handfuls mint leaves, thinly sliced, plus extra to garnish

60 g (2 oz/½ cup) sunflower seeds

250 g (9 oz) haloumi, cut into 5 mm (¼ inch) thick slabs (or use tofu or vegan cheese)

100 g (3½ oz) rocket (arugula) leaves

METHOD:

Heat a barbecue or chargrill pan until very hot. Meanwhile, in a large bowl, toss the zucchini and asparagus with some salt and pepper and about half the olive oil.

Grill the vegetables in batches for 5–10 minutes, until they are cooked through and have some lovely grill marks. Put all the cooked pieces in a large bowl and allow to cool slightly.

While the grilled vegies are still warm, drizzle with the remaining olive oil. Add the onion, garlic, lemon zest and juice, vinegar, chilli flakes and half the mint. Season generosly with salt and cracked pepper. Using your hands, toss the mixture well to ensure the marinade is mixed and each vegetable piece is coated. Set aside to marinate for 20–30 minutes.

Meanwhile, in a dry frying pan over low heat, toast the sunflower seeds, stirring often with a wooden spoon, until they are browned; watch them closely as they can burn quickly. Add a sprinkling of salt and set aside in a small bowl.

Using the same pan over medium heat, drizzle in a little olive oil and add the haloumi slices. Cook for about 1–2 minutes, or until golden brown underneath, then flip and repeat on the other side. Remove the haloumi from the pan and cut into 1 cm (½ inch) strips.

Add the rocket and remaining mint to the salad. Toss to combine and transfer to a serving plate.

Top with the haloumi and toasted sunflower seeds. Serve garnished with a few extra mint leaves and an extra drizzle of olive oil.

ROASTED PUMPKIN WITH TOASTED CRUMBS, MAPLE AND SESAME

This beautiful side dish makes a lovely accompaniment to a range of dishes and styles of food. It's easily one of my favourite ways to eat pumpkin. I personally love roasted pumpkin skin, but you can remove it if you don't. The showering of crumbs over these lovely, dark, roasted pumpkin wedges tends to stick to each piece, giving them a lovely texture.

Serves 8 as a side • vegan, leftovers friendly

INGREDIENTS:

1.5 kg (3 lb 5 oz) jap or kent pumpkin, skin on, cut into 1.5 cm (½ inch) thick wedges

3 tbsp olive oil, plus extra for drizzling

80 ml (2½ fl oz/⅓ cup) maple syrup

80 g (2¾ oz/½ cup) sesame seeds (a mix of black and white if possible)

basil leaves, for serving

Walnut crumbs

2 tbsp olive oil

3 garlic cloves, crushed

60 g (2 oz/½ cup) walnuts, finely chopped

zest of 1 lemon

150 g (5½ oz/2 cups) panko or chunky breadcrumbs (see Note)

1 small handful chopped dill

METHOD:

Preheat the oven to 200°C (400°F). Line two baking trays with baking paper.

Lay the pumpkin wedges over the lined baking trays. Drizzle with the olive oil and sprinkle with salt and pepper. Roast for 20 minutes, or until the pumpkin is beginning to soften and become golden.

Remove the baking trays from the oven and turn the pumpkin wedges over. Drizzle with the maple syrup and a little more oil, then sprinkle with the sesame seeds. Bake for another 8–10 minutes, or until the pumpkin is very golden and soft.

Meanwhile, prepare the crumbs by heating the olive oil in a large, non-stick frying pan over medium heat. Add the garlic and cook for 1 minute, then add the walnuts, lemon zest and breadcrumbs. Cook, stirring for a few minutes, until the mixture turns golden brown. Remove from the heat and allow to cool slightly. Add the dill and season well with salt and pepper.

Arrange the roasted pumpkin in a serving dish and scatter the crumb mixture all over. Serve garnished with basil leaves.

Note: You can make your own panko crumbs by blending some toasted bread in a food processor. This is also a great way to use up bread that's getting stale.

STACKED PASSIONFRUIT AND LEMON PAVLOVA CAKE

This crowd-pleaser is a dessert hybrid—somewhere between a cake, a pavlova and a lemon delicious. The combination of a rich, dense, yet simple cake, crackly meringue, cream and super-zingy curd is just heaven. You can easily use pre-made curd, but I've included my recipe in case you want to go all out and make your own. It's really important to ensure the cake is cooked all the way through—it can be tricky to tell. I like to spoon the meringue not quite to the edge, so there is some cake batter I can test with a skewer.

Makes 1 large cake; serves 10–15

INGREDIENTS:

250 g (9 oz) butter, softened

285 g (10 oz/1¼ cups) caster (superfine) sugar

1 tsp natural vanilla extract

4 eggs

150 g (5½ oz) sour cream

300 g (10½ oz/2 cups) self-raising flour

1 tsp baking powder

300 ml (10 fl oz) cream, whipped

fresh fruit or edible flowers, to garnish

Curd

3 eggs

1 egg yolk

170 g (6 oz/¾ cup) caster (superfine) sugar

100 ml (3½ fl oz) lemon juice

finely grated zest of 2 lemons

pulp of 2 passionfruit, or 50 g (1¾ oz) tinned passionfruit pulp

150 g (5½ oz) butter, softened

Meringue

4 egg whites

pinch of salt

230 g (8 oz/1 cup) caster (superfine) sugar

1 tsp natural vanilla extract

METHOD:

To make the curd, half-fill a small saucepan with water and heat until almost simmering. In a heatproof bowl (one that will fit over the saucepan later on), whisk the eggs, egg yolk and sugar until just combined, then whisk in the lemon juice, lemon zest and passionfruit pulp. Place the bowl over the saucepan, ensuring the base of the bowl isn't touching the water. Gently whisk the mixture to stop the curd cooking too quickly around the edge of the bowl; the mixture should froth, thicken, and turn the consistency of custard or thickened cream. Remove the bowl from the heat. Let the curd cool until just warm, then add the butter a little at a time, whisking well between additions. Cover and refrigerate for at least 1–2 hours, or overnight, to set the curd.

Preheat the oven to 160°C (320°F). Line two 22 cm (9 inch) springform cake tins with baking paper. Using an electric mixer, beat the butter, sugar and vanilla until pale and fluffy. Add the eggs one at a time, beating between additions and scraping down the side of the bowl until incorporated. Don't stress if the cake batter looks like it is beginning to split; it will come back together in the next step.

Beat the sour cream into the egg mixture until combined. Add the flour and baking powder in two batches, folding between additions. Divide the batter evenly among the prepared tins and set aside for the moment.

To make the meringue, whisk the egg whites and salt using an electric mixer set to medium speed. After 3–4 minutes, when the mixture forms soft 'ribbons', gradually add the sugar, a spoonful at a time, whisking until the meringue is very glossy (another 3–4 minutes). In the final minute, add the vanilla.

Spoon half the meringue evenly over each cake and use the back of the spoon to swirl it to cover almost the whole cake tin, leaving a 1–2 cm (½–¾ inch) border. Bake both cakes for 30–40 minutes, or until the meringue is golden brown and the cake batter is set. Allow the cakes to cool completely in their tins.

To assemble, transfer one of the cakes to your serving plate or stand. Spoon a layer of curd evenly over the meringue, spreading it out to about 1 cm (½ inch) from the edge. Spoon on the cream, then spread it over the curd using a spatula.

Gently place the second cake on top. Top with more curd and the remaining cream. Decorate with your favourite fruits or edible flowers.

<u>Note:</u> Save the egg yolks left over from the meringue for making hollandaise sauce or custard, or label and freeze for future baking projects. They'll thaw perfectly well.

LEMON AND ALMOND ITALIAN BISCUITS

These biscuits are the perfect way to finish a night, and equally good for morning or afternoon tea. They are chewy and fragrant, and will store well in a sealed container for up to a week. They make a perfect gift, too, so you'd be wise to double the recipe. Inspired by Ricciarelli biscuits, this version is less sweet, more citrusy, but just as special. Blending whole almonds in a food processor makes for the most amazing chewy texture, but this recipe will also work beautifully with almond meal.

Makes 12–15 biscuits • gluten free, leftovers friendly

INGREDIENTS:

550 g (1 lb 3 oz/3½ cups) raw almonds, or 300 g (10½ oz/3 cups) almond meal

zest of 1 large lemon

115 g (4 oz/½ cup) caster (superfine) sugar

90 g (3 oz/¾ cup) icing (confectioners') sugar, plus extra for coating

2 egg whites

1 tsp natural vanilla extract

12–15 blanched almonds

METHOD:

Preheat the oven to 170°C (340°F) and line a baking tray with baking paper.

If using raw almonds, blend them in a food processor until coarsely ground; some bigger chunks are fine. Set aside.

In a large bowl, combine the lemon zest and sugar by rubbing them together with your fingers until the oils from the lemon zest have released and the mixture is fragrant. Add the icing sugar and blended almonds (or almond meal) and mix well to combine.

In another bowl, beat or whisk the egg whites with a pinch of salt until they form stiff peaks. Mix in the vanilla, then add the egg whites to the sugar mixture. Gently fold together to form a stiff, firm dough.

Tip some extra icing sugar into a small bowl.

Roll the biscuit dough into 12–15 small balls and toss them in the extra icing sugar to coat. Press a blanched almond into each ball, then push them down slightly.

Spread the balls evenly across the lined baking tray and bake for 12 minutes, or until just beginning to colour. Remove the biscuits from the oven and leave to cool and firm up.

The biscuits are delicious warm or at room temperature. Store them in an airtight jar or container.

Chapter Seven

PASTA NIGHT

Ampthill Terrace

AMPTHILL TERRACE:
PASTA NIGHT

Yes, an entire chapter dedicated to pasta—because pasta is so beautifully versatile, nourishing, adaptable and filling. It's the ultimate sharehouse staple, and a perfect meal for a crowd. And a bowl of pasta topped with a delicious sauce also happens to be my favourite food in the whole world! Use these recipes as inspiration, but we all know the best pasta dinner comes from the creative combination of whatever is in your fridge and pantry. We photographed this chapter in a most welcoming Queenslander-style house in Brisbane's Highgate Hill, home to Remi, Marilena, Elia, Lucy and Joe.

Lentil and Mushroom Bolognese

Spring Vegetable Penne with Pea Pesto and Toasted Crumbs

Roasted Pumpkin Mac 'n' Cheese with Walnuts and Sage

Bean Balls in Rich Tomato Sauce

The Creamiest Mixed Mushroom Pasta

Tray Gnocchi with Roasted Tomatoes

The Ultimate Vegetable Lasagne

LENTIL AND MUSHROOM BOLOGNESE

Like so many families, mine ate 'spag bol' at least once a week when I was growing up. It's still one of my favourite pasta dishes. This version is pretty different from a traditional meat sauce in taste and texture, but provides that same familiar, warm, tomatoey flavour. I love the addition of mushrooms, as they give a real heartiness, and the red wine helps bubble up that authentic bolognese aroma. This bolognese is delicious in jaffles, perfect for freezing, and even more flavoursome after a day in the fridge.

Serves 8 • vegan, gluten free, leftovers friendly, freezer friendly

INGREDIENTS:

750 ml (25½ fl oz/3 cups) vegetable stock (see Note)

500 g (1 lb 2 oz/2 cups) dried split red lentils (see Note)

2 tbsp olive oil, plus extra for drizzling

1 large brown onion, diced

2 carrots, finely diced

2 celery stalks, finely diced

4 garlic cloves, crushed

300 g (10½ oz) mushrooms, diced

2 tsp dried oregano

2 tsp dried basil

2 × 400 g (14 oz) tins good-quality tomatoes (I love cherry tomatoes in this recipe)

125 ml (4 fl oz/½ cup) red wine

2 tsp caster (superfine) sugar

500 g (1 lb 2 oz) pasta of your choice

grated parmesan (or vegan cheese/ nutritional yeast), to serve

basil leaves, to serve

METHOD:

Heat the stock in a saucepan until warm, then add the dried lentils. Bring to the boil and cook until all the water is absorbed and the lentils are soft; this usually only takes about 10–20 minutes, so keep an eye on them.

Meanwhile, in a large saucepan, heat the olive oil and fry the onion over medium heat for a few minutes, stirring often. Add the carrots and celery, along with an extra swig of olive oil and a pinch of salt. Cook for about 10–20 minutes, stirring every couple of minutes until the vegies are browning and reduced. Don't worry if they're sticking to the pan a little.

Stir in the garlic, mushrooms and dried herbs and cook for another 5 minutes.

Add the cooked lentils to the pan, along with the tinned tomatoes, wine and sugar, then stir to combine. Reduce the heat to low and simmer, stirring occasionally to prevent sticking, for about 30 minutes, until the sauce has thickened and deepened in colour. Season the sauce to taste.

While the sauce is simmering, cook the pasta in a large saucepan of boiling, salted water until *al dente*.

Serve the pasta topped with the bolognese sauce, grated parmesan and basil leaves.

<u>Notes:</u> Homemade stock is great, if you happen to have some. Alternatively, you can dissolve 2 stock cubes in 750 ml (25½ fl oz/3 cups) water.

You can use tinned lentils if you like. They change the texture significantly, but are equally delicious. Replace the red lentils and stock with 3 × 400 g (14 oz) tins of drained brown lentils, and add them with the tinned tomatoes.

SPRING VEGETABLE PENNE WITH PEA PESTO AND TOASTED CRUMBS

This pasta is wonderfully fresh and super flexible. It's a lovely, quick recipe too, all coming together in the time it takes to cook the pasta. Peas make a great addition to the pesto because they're inexpensive, complement the herbs, and provide an almost creamy texture; instead of the pine nuts in the pesto, you can also use cashews, almonds or walnuts. And don't be afraid to work with whatever vegies you have on hand: broccolini, mushrooms, sugar snap peas and spinach would all be great tossed through the pasta. Just be careful to avoid overcooking the vegetables, to ensure they remain vibrant. The crunchy topping is a wonderful vegan addition to lots of pastas, salads and baked dishes.

Serves 6–8 • vegan, gluten-free option, leftovers friendly

SPRING VEGETABLE PENNE WITH PEA PESTO AND TOASTED CRUMBS

INGREDIENTS:

500 g (1 lb 2 oz) penne

2 tbsp olive oil

2 large zucchini (courgettes), cut into thin moons

1 bunch asparagus, cut into thin spear shapes

185 g (6½ oz/1 cup) shelled broad (fava) beans

1 bunch spring onions (scallions), chopped

½ bunch kale, finely chopped

250 ml (8½ fl oz/1 cup) vegetable stock

250 g (9 oz) frozen peas

Pesto

500 g (1 lb 2 oz) fresh or frozen peas, cooked

50 g (1¾ oz/⅓ cup) pine nuts, toasted

3 garlic cloves, peeled

1 bunch basil, leaves picked

½ bunch mint, leaves picked

zest and juice of 1 lemon

125 ml (4 fl oz/½ cup) olive oil

30 g (1 oz/½ cup) nutritional yeast; or 100 g (3½ oz/1 cup) grated parmesan for non-vegans

1 tsp salt

Toasted Crumbs

2 tbsp olive oil

120 g (4½ oz/2 cups) chunky breadcrumbs (panko or homemade)

zest of 1 lemon

3 garlic cloves, crushed

METHOD:

Put all the pesto ingredients in a blender. Add 3 tablespoons water and blend until smooth and creamy. Season to taste and set aside.

Bring a large saucepan of salted water to the boil. Cook the penne until *al dente*, then drain well, reserving 125 ml (4 fl oz/½ cup) of the cooking water.

Meanwhile, in a large frying pan, heat the olive oil over high heat. Add the zucchini and cook for a few minutes, stirring every so often. Add the asparagus, broad beans and spring onions. Cook for a minute, then add the kale, stock and frozen peas. Season with salt and pepper, bring to a simmer, then turn off the heat. Pour the pesto in and stir well to combine.

For the toasted crumbs, heat the olive oil in a non-stick frying pan over medium heat. Add the breadcrumbs, lemon zest and garlic. Cook, stirring for a few minutes, until the crumbs are a deep golden colour. Season well and set aside.

Combine the pasta, reserved pasta water and pesto vegetable mix. Serve in bowls, topped with toasted breadcrumbs, and extra herbs and cheese if desired.

ROASTED PUMPKIN MAC 'N' CHEESE
WITH WALNUTS AND SAGE

Slow-cooked caramelised onion, roasted pumpkin and a hint of spice give this mac 'n' cheese a subtle sweetness, with crunchy walnuts and crispy sage making it just a little bit more special. The flavour combination is perfect. The trick to making this dish super delicious is to roast the pumpkin until it is brown and very soft, and to caramelise the onions properly— be patient! This version contains a lot of sauce, as the pasta tends to soak up a lot of liquid while it is being finished off in the oven.

Serves 8 • vegan option

INGREDIENTS:

1.5 kg (3 lb 5 oz) butternut pumpkin (squash), cut into 2 cm (¾ inch) chunks

3 tbsp olive oil, plus extra for drizzling

2 large brown onions, sliced

25 g (1 oz) butter or margarine

500 g (1 lb 2 oz) macaroni or curly pasta

3 tbsp plain (all-purpose) flour

½ tsp ground nutmeg

1 tsp dried tarragon

375 ml (12½ fl oz/1½ cups) milk (or nut milk)

500 ml (17 fl oz/2 cups) vegetable stock

60 g (2 oz/½ cup) grated cheddar (or vegan cheese/nutritional yeast), plus extra for topping

25 g (1 oz/¼ cup) grated parmesan (or vegan cheese/nutritional yeast)

1 handful sage leaves, thinly sliced

60 g (2 oz/½ cup) walnuts, roughly chopped

METHOD:

Preheat the oven to 220°C (430°F). Arrange the pumpkin chunks on a large baking tray. Drizzle with 2 tablespoons of the olive oil, and sprinkle with salt and pepper. Roast for about 20–30 minutes, or until soft to touch and dark brown in colour.

Meanwhile, in a saucepan, heat the remaining olive oil over low heat and slowly caramelise the onions, stirring often, for about 15 minutes, until browned. Stir in the butter, cook for a few minutes more, then set aside.

While the onions are slowly caramelising, cook the pasta in a large saucepan of salted, boiling water until almost *al dente*, but drain it 1–2 minutes before you normally would, as it will continue to soften in the oven. Drain the pasta in a colander, run cold water over it and set aside.

Add the flour, nutmeg and tarragon to the caramelised onion mixture and stir well. Pour in the milk and stock, and stir the sauce until it comes to a simmer and begins to thicken. Add the roasted pumpkin and mix well.

Using a stick blender, whiz the onion and pumpkin mixture until it is completely smooth. Alternatively, you could transfer the mixture to a food processor or blender.

Add the cheddar and parmesan to the sauce and stir until melted. Taste and season to your liking.

Combine the pasta and sauce in a large baking dish. Top with the sage, walnuts and extra cheddar. Drizzle with more olive oil and sprinkle with salt and pepper.

Bake for 10 minutes, or until the cheddar is melted and the sage is crispy. Serve garnished with fresh herbs if desired.

BEAN BALLS IN RICH TOMATO SAUCE

These 'meatballs' are delicious over spaghetti, and are also great in a crunchy bread roll with some melted mozzarella or vegan cheese, or over polenta. The ultimate comfort food, they are full of flavour yet simple to make. I won't pretend they taste like meatballs, but these bean balls do bear a creditable resemblance.

The bean balls do take a bit of time because you need to roast the eggplant. However, this can be done well ahead, or you can replace the eggplant with about 1 cup of smoked eggplant from a jar or deli counter. I like the flavour combo of black beans and kidney beans, which also makes the balls look very 'meaty', but you could use lentils or other beans depending on what you have on hand. Instead of chopping the garlic and mashing the bean ball mixture by hand, you can save a bit of time and effort by just whizzing it all up together in a food processor.

Makes 24 bean balls in sauce; serves 6 • vegan, gluten-free option

BEAN BALLS IN RICH TOMATO SAUCE

INGREDIENTS:

Bean Balls

1 large eggplant (aubergine)

400 g (14 oz) tin kidney beans, drained

400 g (14 oz) tin black beans, drained

3 garlic cloves, crushed

2 tbsp olive oil

1 tsp smoked paprika

80 ml (2½ fl oz/⅓ cup) tomato passata (puréed tomatoes), from a 700 g (1 lb 9 oz) jar; reserve the remaining passata for making the sauce

1 tsp dried basil

1 tbsp chia seeds, combined in a small bowl with 3 tbsp boiling water

75 g (2¾ oz/½ cup) plain (all-purpose) flour (or gluten-free flour), plus extra for dusting

150 g (5½ oz/1½ cups) breadcrumbs (or use gluten-free)

Rich Tomato Sauce

1 tbsp olive oil

1 large brown onion, diced

4 garlic cloves, crushed

1 tsp dried basil

2 × 400 g (14 oz) tins chopped tomatoes

700 g (1 lb 9 oz) jar passata (minus the 4 tbsp used in the bean balls)

2 tsp sugar

METHOD:

Preheat the oven to 200°C (400°F). Place the whole eggplant on a baking tray and roast for 1 hour, turning halfway through, until the eggplant smells smoky, the flesh is super soft and the skin feels crisp. Remove from the oven and allow to cool.

In a large bowl, mash the kidney and black beans together with a fork until almost smooth (some chunks are fine). Cut the cooled eggplant in half and use a spoon to scoop out the flesh, adding it to the bean mix. Add all the remaining bean ball ingredients and stir well until smooth and combined. The mixture will be quite wet, but this will ensure moist bean balls.

Use your hands, dusted with flour, to roll the mixture into 24 balls, about the size of golf balls. Lightly coat each ball with a dusting of flour, to ensure they hold their shape during cooking.

Transfer the balls to a lined baking tray and bake for 20–30 minutes, or until they have firmed slightly and are beginning to colour.

While the balls are in the oven, make the sauce. Heat the olive oil in a heavy-based saucepan, add the onion and cook over medium heat for about 5–10 minutes, or until golden and translucent. Add the garlic and basil, along with a sprinkle of salt and pepper, and cook for a further few minutes.

Add the remaining sauce ingredients and 500 ml (17 fl oz/2 cups) water and turn the heat up to high. Allow the sauce to come to the boil, then reduce the heat to low and cook for 15 minutes or so. The sauce is ready when it has thickened and is a darker shade of red. Taste and add more seasoning if needed.

Once the bean balls are done, gently add them, a few at a time, into the sauce. Use a spoon to coat the balls in sauce as you go.

Serve as desired: with cooked spaghetti, polenta, roasted potatoes or in a toasted bread roll.

THE CREAMIEST MIXED MUSHROOM PASTA

Look, this recipe won't win any health awards, but sometimes we just need to indulge—and this is one of my favourite ways to do just that. Real egg pasta is essential. It's also really important to cook the mushrooms in a big frying pan over high heat, giving them room to caramelise and to ensure they don't sweat. If you don't have an appropriate pan, cook them in two batches. I love the addition of the crispy king oyster mushrooms on top, but you could replace these with pine nuts, toasted crumbs or cheese.

Serves 5–6 • gluten-free option, leftovers friendly

INGREDIENTS:

1 tbsp olive oil

1 brown onion, thinly sliced

100 g (3½ oz) butter

500 g (1 lb 2 oz) mixed mushrooms, sliced (I used button and Swiss browns)

5 garlic cloves, crushed

2 tsp chopped thyme, or 1 tsp dried

150 g (5½ oz) oyster or king oyster mushrooms, stems removed, cut into matchsticks

400 g (14 oz) fresh egg pasta (or gluten-free pasta)

190 ml (6½ fl oz/¾ cup) white wine

125 ml (4 fl oz/½ cup) vegetable stock

300 ml (10 fl oz) pouring (single/light) cream

200 g (7 oz) baby spinach leaves

100 g (3½ oz/1 cup) grated parmesan, plus extra for serving

basil leaves, to serve

METHOD:

In a large frying pan, heat the olive oil over medium heat. Add the onion and cook slowly, stirring often, for about 10 minutes, or until the onion is browning and significantly reduced.

Add 75 g (2¾ oz) of the butter to the pan and turn the heat to high. Add the mushrooms and let them cook and sweat out their liquid, stirring only every minute or so, until they begin to brown. If your pan isn't very big, cook the mushrooms in two batches. After about 5 minutes of cooking, add the garlic and thyme and continue to cook for a further 5 minutes.

Meanwhile, bring a large saucepan of salted water to the boil, ready for the pasta. In another non-stick frying pan, melt the remaining butter. Once it starts sizzling, add the king oyster mushroom strips. Cook for 5 minutes or so, stirring infrequently, until the strips have shrunk and are golden brown and beginning to crisp up. Season well and set aside.

After the mixed mushrooms have been cooking for around 10 minutes and are looking brown and delicious, put the pasta on to cook, stirring regularly.

Reduce the frying pan heat to low and add the wine and stock to the mixed mushrooms, deglazing the pan and stirring for about 2 minutes, or until about half the wine has evaporated. Stir in the cream, along with salt and pepper to taste. Bring to a gentle simmer and stir in the spinach and parmesan. Continue to simmer gently until the pasta is ready.

Once the pasta is *al dente*, drain the pasta, reserving 125 ml (4 fl oz/½ cup) of the cooking water. Add the pasta water and pasta to the frying pan with the sauce. Stir carefully to combine, still over a low heat. Taste and season if necessary.

Serve immediately, topped with the king oyster mushroom strips, extra parmesan and fresh basil.

TRAY GNOCCHI WITH ROASTED TOMATOES

Homemade gnocchi is a lovely dish for a special occasion. However, the store-bought stuff is a great substitute, and makes this dish super 'hands off' to prepare. I love these homemade gnocchi with fragrant, chunky, roasted tomatoes, but they're also delicious with lots of different sauces. Frying the gnocchi after they've been boiled isn't essential, but I'm really into the crispy outer texture that a little sizzle gives them. The whole dish can be made ahead of time, and simply reheated in the same baking dish used to roast the tomatoes in. It's lovely finished with some parmesan or soft feta, and accompanied by some fresh greens.

Serves 6 • vegan

INGREDIENTS:

Roasted Tomatoes

600 g (1 lb 5 oz) cherry tomatoes, in mixed colours if available

200 g (7 oz) truss tomatoes, quartered

1 red onion, sliced into thin strips

3 tbsp olive oil

8 garlic cloves, skin on

1 handful rosemary leaves

1 large handful basil leaves, plus extra to serve

Gnocchi
(or use 500 g/1 lb 2 oz packet gnocchi)

1.5 kg (3 lb 5 oz) kipfler (fingerling) potatoes, peeled

3 tbsp olive oil, plus extra for pan-frying

350 g (12½ oz/2⅓ cups) plain (all-purpose) flour, plus extra for dusting

METHOD:

Preheat the oven to 200°C (400°F). To roast the tomatoes, place them in a large baking dish with the onion and olive oil. Toss well to coat, season with salt and pepper and roast for 20 minutes. Remove the baking dish from the oven, turn the tomatoes, and add the garlic cloves and rosemary. Roast for another 20 minutes, or until the garlic is soft and the tomatoes are shrivelled and golden. Squeeze the garlic cloves out of their skins (let them cool a bit first as they'll be hot), then toss the softened cloves as well as most of the fresh basil with the tomatoes. Discard the garlic skin and reserve a few basil leaves for garnishing.

Meanwhile, make a start on the gnocchi. Place the potatoes in a saucepan of cold water and bring to the boil. Cook for 15 minutes, or until tender when tested with a fork. Drain completely, then return the potatoes to the pan over low heat and toss for a minute to remove the moisture. Add the olive oil and mash well until the potato is smooth and all the lumps have been removed. Add the flour and mix well to combine. Taste the gnocchi dough and ensure it's seasoned well.

On a lightly floured surface, roll the dough into long rolls about 2 cm (¾ inch) thick. Use a sharp knife to cut each roll into 1 cm (½ inch) pieces.

Bring a large saucepan of salted water to the boil. Once the water is bubbling, gently add one-third of the gnocchi pieces. After about a minute, when the gnocchi rise to the surface, remove them with a slotted spoon and allow to cool on a tray. Cook the remaining two batches of gnocchi in the same way and allow to cool.

Heat a large, non-stick frying pan over medium heat with an extra drizzle of olive oil. Fry the gnocchi in two batches, cooking on each side for a few minutes until golden and crisp.

Add the gnocchi to the roasted tomato mixture and season to taste. Garnish with basil and serve.

THE ULTIMATE VEGETABLE LASAGNE

A wise addition to your shared cooking repertoire, this lasagne is a real crowd-pleaser.
Layers of roasted vegetables, mushroom ragu and pumpkin béchamel sauce make
this lasagne seriously special. All the layers do involve a bit of work, so I usually
prepare a huge quantity to feed a crowd. The lasagne is even better the next day.

Serves 10 • vegan option, leftovers friendly

INGREDIENTS:

3 eggplants (aubergines), cut into 1 cm
(½ inch) slabs

4 zucchini (courgettes), cut lengthways
into 5 mm (¼ inch) slabs

olive oil, for drizzling

500 g (1 lb 2 oz) lasagne sheets

200 g (7 oz) baby spinach leaves

125 g (4½ oz/1 cup) grated cheddar
(or nutritional yeast)

50 g (1¾ oz/½ cup) grated parmesan
(or nutritional yeast)

Mushroom Ragu

300 g (10½ oz) button mushrooms

200 g (7 oz) Swiss brown mushrooms

2 tbsp olive oil

1 brown onion, diced

1 carrot, finely diced

5 garlic cloves, chopped

2 tsp dried thyme

1 tsp dried basil

700 g (1 lb 9 oz) jar tomato passata
(puréed tomatoes)

400 g (14 oz) tin chopped tomatoes

Pumpkin Béchamel

500 g (1 lb 2 oz) pumpkin (winter
squash), cut into 3 cm (1¼ inch) cubes

2 tbsp olive oil

3 tbsp butter (or vegan margarine)

3 tbsp plain (all-purpose) flour

750 ml (25½ fl oz/3 cups) milk
(or nut milk)

½ tsp grated nutmeg

METHOD:

To make the ragu, dice the mushrooms and set aside. Heat the olive oil in a large, heavy-based saucepan, add the onion and carrot and cook over low heat, stirring often, for 15 minutes. Turn the heat up to medium and add the mushrooms, garlic, thyme and basil, cooking for another 5 minutes. Add the passata, tomatoes and seasoning, along with about 125–250 ml (4–8½ fl oz/½–1 cup) water, from rinsing out the passata jar and tomato tin. Bring the sauce to a simmer, then reduce the heat and allow it to bubble for at least 30 minutes, and up to 2 hours.

Meanwhile, preheat the oven to 200°C (400°F). Place the pumpkin pieces for the béchamel on a baking tray, drizzle with the olive oil and roast until soft and brown. Mash the pumpkin until smooth, or process in a blender, then set aside.

While the pumpkin is roasting, spread some of the eggplant and zucchini slices on a separate tray. Drizzle with a little olive oil, season each piece and bake for 20 minutes, or until soft and turning golden. Repeat with all the eggplant and zucchini. (You can also cook them on a grill if you prefer.)

To make the béchamel, melt the butter in a small saucepan until bubbling. Add the flour and whisk to combine for 1 minute. Slowly pour in half the milk, whisking to combine into a smooth sauce, then slowly whisk in the remaining milk. Continue whisking until the sauce thickens. Add the nutmeg and blended pumpkin. Stir well, then taste and adjust the salt and pepper quantities.

To assemble the lasagne, spread a few spoonfuls of ragu in the base of a large, deep baking dish. Cover with a single layer of lasagne sheets. Top with another 1 cm (½ inch) layer of ragu, a few handfuls of spinach leaves, a layer of roasted eggplant and zucchini, followed by the béchamel sauce. Layer more lasagne sheets on top.

Repeat once or twice to make another layer of all the fillings; the number of layers will depend on the size of your dish. Finish the lasagne with pasta sheets and top with a final layer of béchamel sauce.

Sprinkle the cheddar and parmesan on top and bake for 40 minutes, or until golden. Serve garnished with fresh herbs if desired.

Chapter Eight

COMFORT FOOD SPREAD

WELLINGTON ROAD:
COMFORT FOOD SPREAD

Comfort food … is food so delicious it cheers your soul. There's nothing like culinary nostalgia to warm the cockles of your heart, and so the following menu is inspired by childhood classics and all-time crowd favourites, drawing heavily on those classic comfort ingredients, pastry, butter and cheese. We photographed this chapter in a long-standing sharehouse in East Brisbane, home to Ella, Sid, Adam … and Manny the dog, Ella's most reliable partner in crime.

Baked Caramelised Onion and Cheese Fondue

Creamy Mushroom and Spinach Pies with Homemade Cheddar Crust

Walnut, Apple and Sage 'Sausage' Rolls

Avocado and Kale Caesar Salad

Curried Lentil Shepherd's Pie with Sweet Potato Top

Apple and Pear Crumble

Sticky Date Cake with Salted Caramel Sauce and Burnt Sugar Figs

Peanut Butter and Honey Brownies

BAKED CARAMELISED ONION AND CHEESE FONDUE

This decadent dish is the ultimate party starter for an indulgent crowd. I love the combination of the super-tender onions with thyme—it's a little reminiscent of French onion soup. Using a bitey cheddar makes it really special, but you can be flexible and use a variety of cheeses such as crumbled goat's cheese, feta, grated mozzarella or gruyère. Serve the fondue with some crusty fresh bread.

Serves 8–10 as a starter • gluten free, leftovers friendly, freezer friendly

INGREDIENTS:

75 g (2¾ oz) butter

1 tbsp olive oil

3 brown onions, very thinly sliced

250 g (9 oz/1 cup) sour cream

250 g (9 oz/2 cups) grated vintage cheddar

100 g (3½ oz) soft goat's cheese, broken into little pieces

3 garlic cloves, thinly sliced

1 tbsp thyme leaves, or 2 tsp dried thyme, plus extra sprigs to serve

3 tbsp worcestershire sauce

50 g (1¾ oz/½ cup) grated parmesan

METHOD:

Heat the butter and olive oil in a heavy-based saucepan over medium heat. Add the onions, sprinkle with salt and pepper and cook for about 5 minutes. Reduce the heat to low and cook for a further 20 minutes, stirring every now and then.

Meanwhile, preheat the oven to 200°C (400°F). Combine the sour cream, cheddar and goat's cheese in an ovenproof bowl or dish and set aside.

Once the caramelised onions are deep brown and silky soft, add the garlic and cook for another few minutes. Add the thyme and worcestershire sauce and mix well.

Add the onion mixture to the bowl with the sour cream and cheese. Mix well to combine. Sprinkle the parmesan on top and season with salt and pepper.

Bake for 10 minutes, or until all the cheese is melted, bubbling and golden. Sprinkle with the extra thyme and serve warm, with bread.

Wellington Road: Comfort Food Spread   Page 191

CREAMY MUSHROOM AND SPINACH PIES WITH HOMEMADE CHEDDAR CRUST

This recipe can be used to make two large round pies, a heap of individual pies in muffin tins, or more rustic (read: less fiddly) flat tortes, as pictured here. Making your own pastry can be daunting, but if you've never done it before, this cheddar-laden version is a great place to begin. After all, who is going to notice a slightly-less-than-perfect texture if it tastes like cheesy goodness? The number one thing to remember with pastry is to keep it as cold as possible—so making sure all your ingredients are chilled is crucial, and so is working quickly when you're assembling everything.

———— Makes 2 large pies, or about 18 muffin-sized pies • vegan option, leftovers friendly, freezer friendly ————

CREAMY MUSHROOM AND SPINACH PIES WITH HOMEMADE CHEDDAR CRUST

INGREDIENTS:

Pastry
(or replace with 6 sheets of vegan puff pastry)

125 g (4½ oz) cheddar, cut into 1 cm (½ inch) cubes

120 g (4½ oz) chilled butter, cut into 1 cm (½ inch) cubes

375 g (13 oz/2½ cups) plain (all-purpose) flour, plus extra for dusting

1 tsp salt

1 egg yolk

170 ml (5½ fl oz/⅔ cup) iced water

1 egg, whisked, for brushing (or use melted margarine)

Filling

2 tbsp olive oil

1 large brown onion, diced

1 leek, sliced into moons (I use the whole leek; just wash the top bit really well)

700 g (1 lb 9 oz) button mushrooms, halved/quartered depending on size

50 g (1¾ oz) butter (or margarine)

4 garlic cloves, crushed

2 tsp dried tarragon

1 tsp dried thyme

2 vegetable stock (bouillon) cubes

2 tbsp plain (all-purpose) flour

1 tbsp tomato paste (concentrated purée)

3 tbsp worcestershire sauce

1 tsp salt

200 g (7 oz) chopped spinach (I use frozen)

125 g (4 oz/½ cup) sour cream (or nut milk plus 2 tbsp nutritional yeast)

METHOD:

To make the pastry, put the cheese, butter, flour and salt in a large bowl. Rub together with your fingertips, to break the butter and cheese into smaller pieces while incorporating them into the flour. (You can also do this with a few quick pulses in a food processor.) You want to end up with a chunky breadcrumb consistency. Some big chunks are absolutely fine; they will melt and become little pockets of flavour in your pastry.

Add the egg yolk and iced water, and use a fork to mix the dough together. Bring the pastry into a ball with your hands, then transfer to a bowl, cover with a clean cloth and place in the fridge. Let it sit there and rest while you make the filling.

Heat the olive oil in a large, heavy-based saucepan. Add the onion and leek. Cook over medium heat for 10 minutes, stirring often. Add the mushrooms, butter and garlic, along with a sprinkle of salt. Cook, stirring only every 2 minutes, for about 10 minutes, or until the mushrooms are golden and reduced.

Add the herbs, stock cubes, flour and tomato paste and stir well to combine. After a minute or two, add the worcestershire sauce, salt, spinach and sour cream, along with 125 ml (4 fl oz/½ cup) water. Stir well and cook until the spinach has wilted or thawed.

Cool the filling, by either setting aside for an hour, or refrigerating for 20 minutes.

Preheat the oven to 200°C (400°F). Line two baking trays with baking paper.

Cut the pastry into four chunks. On a well-floured surface, roll each pastry portion out to a thin, roughly circular sheet using a rolling pin. Make two circles about 25–30 cm (10–12 inches) in diameter for the pie bases, and two circles about 20 cm (8 inches) in diameter for the lids.

Carefully transfer the larger pastry circles to the lined baking trays. Don't stress if there are some tears or holes; just patch them up with more dough. Spoon the filling onto each circle, in the centre, leaving a pastry border of about 3 cm (1¼ inches).

Lay the smaller pastry circles over the top. Carefully use the overhanging pastry to create folds all around the perimeter of each pie, or simply fold it up and press together with a fork. Any leftover pastry can be frozen for later use.

Brush the top of the pies with the whisked egg. Bake for 30 minutes, or until the pies are golden and all the pastry is cooked through.

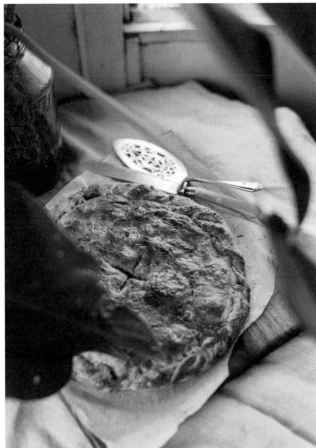

WALNUT, APPLE AND SAGE 'SAUSAGE' ROLLS

A few years before I stopped cooking meat, I would make pork, apple and fennel sausage rolls and take them to just about every house party or social event, because they were so well loved and requested. I've quietly subbed in these vegan ones now, and while they taste a little different, the requests keep coming.

I make them using textured vegetable protein (TVP), which, if you've never cooked with it before, will rock your world! It soaks up whatever liquid it is cooked in, so it's the perfect vessel for any flavourful sauce. It is very inexpensive and can be bought in bulk and stored forever. You'll find it in most good health food shops, but if you can't track it down, just use 300 g (10½ oz) vegan mince or crumbled firm tofu and leave out the stock.

Makes 30 party-sized sausage rolls • vegan, leftovers friendly, freezer friendly

INGREDIENTS:

3 sheets vegan puff pastry

3 tbsp nut milk of choice
(or 1 egg, beaten)

fennel seeds, for sprinkling (optional)

tomato sauce or chutney, to serve

'Sausage' Mince

2 tbsp olive oil

1 brown onion, finely diced

3 garlic cloves, crushed

85 g (3 oz/⅔ cup) walnuts, finely chopped

10 sage leaves, finely sliced

1 apple, grated

1 tbsp worcestershire sauce

1 tbsp soy sauce

1 tsp smoked paprika

1 tsp dried thyme leaves

3 tbsp nutritional yeast

90 g (3 oz/1 cup) dried TVP (textured vegetable protein)

375 ml (12½ fl oz/1½ cups) vegetable stock

100 g (3½ oz/1 cup) breadcrumbs

3 tbsp finely chopped parsley (optional)

METHOD:

To prepare the 'sausage' mince, heat the olive oil in a large, heavy-based saucepan. Add the onion and cook over low heat for about 10 minutes, stirring often, until browned and translucent. Add the garlic, walnuts and sage, along with a little salt and some cracked pepper. Cook for a further few minutes. Stir in the apple, worcestershire sauce, soy sauce, paprika, thyme and nutritional yeast and turn the heat up to medium. Cook for a few minutes, until searing hot.

Add the TVP and stock and stir well to combine. Bring the mixture to a simmer and cook for 2–3 minutes, to give the TVP a chance to soak up the liquid.

Turn the heat off and add the breadcrumbs, and parsley if using. Stir well to combine. Taste the mixture and add seasoning to taste. Let the mixture cool for about 30 minutes, until cool enough to handle.

Preheat the oven to 180°C (350°F). Line a large baking tray with baking paper.

Cut each sheet of pastry in half to make two rectangles. Place one-sixth of the filling mixture in the centre of each piece of pastry, shaping it into a long sausage lengthways down the pastry sheet. Firmly fold over the pastry sheet, and in one swift movement, roll it into a tight long roll, so the edge is on the bottom.

Repeat with all the remaining pastry and filling.

Cut each roll into five equal pieces (or into two for larger rolls). Lay them on the baking tray with a little space between each one. Brush a little nut milk onto each roll and sprinkle with fennel seeds, if desired.

Bake for 20 minutes, or until the pastry is golden and puffy. Serve warm, with tomato sauce or chutney.

AVOCADO AND KALE CAESAR SALAD

This salad is the perfect side for lots of meals, and hearty enough to be a meal on its own. If you don't cook with kale much, note that the process of 'massaging' it with your hands makes all the difference to its overall flavour and texture. (Be sure to massage kale with a little dressing any time you're eating it raw!) If you want to omit the soft-boiled eggs, grilled mushrooms are a lovely replacement. The croutons are a great way to use bread that's a bit stale; I often freeze the stale 'heel' of my weekly loaf, to thaw and toast whenever I need croutons. If you're keeping the salad vegan, sun-dried tomato strips make a lovely salty element in place of the shaved parmesan.

Serves 4–6 • vegan option, gluten-free option

INGREDIENTS:

3 thick slices sourdough bread, cut into 2 cm (¾ inch) cubes

2 tbsp olive oil

4 eggs (omit for vegan)

1 bunch kale, stems removed, leaves chopped (about 5 cups)

50 g (1¾ oz/½ cup) shaved parmesan (omit for vegan)

½ large avocado, sliced

Dressing

½ large avocado, flesh chopped

2 small garlic cloves, peeled

juice of 1 lime

1 tbsp olive oil

1 tbsp tahini

3 tbsp vegan mayonnaise

1 tsp dijon mustard

2 tsp worcestershire sauce

2 tsp Tabasco or other hot sauce

½ tsp salt

METHOD:

Preheat the oven to 180°C (350°F). Arrange the bread cubes on a baking tray and drizzle with the olive oil. Sprinkle with salt and pepper, then bake for 15–20 minutes, turning halfway through. The croutons are done when they are golden and crunchy.

Meanwhile, gently place the eggs in a small saucepan and cover with water. Bring the water to the boil over medium heat. Once boiling, turn the heat off and leave the eggs for 4–5 minutes. Drain the hot water and immediately transfer the eggs to a bowl of cold water. Once they're cool enough to handle, peel the eggs and set aside.

Place all the dressing ingredients in a blender. Add 3 tablespoons water and blend together. Taste and adjust the seasoning to your liking.

Place the kale in a large bowl, sprinkle with salt and drizzle half the dressing over. Use your hands to massage the kale with the dressing for about a minute. Add the parmesan, avocado, croutons and remaining dressing and toss well to combine.

Transfer the salad to a serving plate. Halve the eggs, arrange on top and serve.

CURRIED LENTIL SHEPHERD'S PIE WITH SWEET POTATO TOP

Warm, simple and so very comforting—who doesn't crave a good hearty pie every so often? Curry powder, mustard seeds and coconut give this one a lovely subtle curry aroma, but you could also flavour the filling with other herbs and spices you have on hand. The flavour is even better a day or so after making the pie, so it's a great meal to cook up on the weekend to keep you going on busy weeknights.

Serves 8 • vegan, gluten free, leftovers friendly, freezer friendly

INGREDIENTS:

700 g (1 lb 9 oz) starchy potatoes, peeled and cut into 2 cm (¾ inch) cubes

700 g (1 lb 9 oz) sweet potatoes, peeled and cut into 2 cm (¾ inch) cubes

3 tbsp olive oil

400 ml (14 fl oz) tin coconut milk

1 large brown onion, diced

3 carrots, diced

3 celery stalks, diced

300 g (10½ oz) mushrooms, diced

4 garlic cloves, crushed

2 tsp mustard seeds

1 tbsp curry powder

2 tbsp worcestershire sauce

3 × 400 g (14 oz) tins brown lentils

400 g (14 oz) tin chopped tomatoes

300 g (10½ oz/2 cups) frozen peas

½ bunch dill, chopped

fresh herbs, black sesame seeds or crispy fried onions, to serve (optional)

METHOD:

Place the potato and sweet potato cubes in a large saucepan and cover with cold water. Bring to the boil over medium heat and cook until the vegetables are soft and tender. Drain off the water. Add half the olive oil to the pan, along with one-third of the coconut milk and a generous seasoning of salt and pepper. Mash the mixture until smooth, then set aside.

Meanwhile, heat the remaining olive oil in a large saucepan. Add the onion, carrots and celery, season with salt and pepper and cook for 10 minutes over medium heat, stirring often. Once the vegetables are browning and tender, add the mushrooms, garlic, mustard seeds and curry powder. Cook, stirring often, for another 5–10 minutes.

Add the worcestershire sauce, lentils (including the liquid in the tins), tomatoes and remaining coconut milk. Bring the mixture to a simmer and cook for 10–15 minutes, or until thick and aromatic. Turn off the heat, then add the peas and dill and mix to combine.

Pour the lentil mixture into a large baking dish. Spoon the sweet potato mixture over the top and use a spatula to spread it almost to the edges.

Bake for 20 minutes, or until the topping is golden. Serve sprinkled with fresh herbs, sesame seeds or crispy fried onions if desired.

APPLE AND PEAR CRUMBLE

Apple crumble is an absolute staple in my family. Some of my earliest cooking memories are of learning to rub butter, sugar and flour together to form the all-important breadcrumb-like mix with Grandma, as we prepared massive crumbles for the whole family. I've strayed from the traditional family recipe here, but it still retains the nostalgia of the simple classic. Stewing your own apples and pears is a lovely touch, and in my opinion really makes this crumble sing. Reserve the excess stewing liquid and use it in other cooking; it's delicious as a syrup for sodas, or mixed into cakes or muffins. However, you can of course use tinned apples and pears if you're short on time.

Serves 8–10 • vegan option, leftovers friendly

INGREDIENTS:

110 g (4 oz/½ cup) sugar

1 cinnamon stick, or 1 tsp ground cinnamon

1 tsp cloves

2 tsp natural vanilla extract

2 tbsp lemon juice

6 cooking pears, peeled and quartered, cores removed (bosc and anjou pears work well)

6 green apples, peeled and quartered, cores removed

Crumble

100 g (3½ oz) chilled butter, cut into 1 cm (½ inch) pieces (or use vegan margarine)

165 g (6 oz/¾ cup) brown sugar

150 g (5½ oz/1 cup) plain (all-purpose) flour

150 g (5½ oz/1½ cups) rolled (porridge) oats

30 g (1 oz/¼ cup) slivered almonds

½ tsp ground cinnamon

METHOD:

Put the sugar, spices, vanilla and lemon juice into a large saucepan. Add 1 litre (34 fl oz/4 cups) water and whisk well over medium heat. Now add the fruit. The liquid should be just covering the fruit, so add a little extra water if necessary. Bring to the boil, then cover the pan and reduce the heat to low. Simmer for 30 minutes, or until the fruit is pierced easily with a fork. Discard the spices. Drain the fruit, reserving at least 250 ml (8½ fl oz/1 cup) of the stewing liquid for the crumble; you can keep the rest of the stewing liquid for other uses. Set the stewed fruit aside.

Meanwhile, make the crumble. Combine the butter, sugar and flour in a large bowl. Rub the mixture with your fingertips until it has a breadcrumb-like texture. Add the oats, almonds and cinnamon and mix again with your fingertips until everything is combined well. Store the mixture in the fridge until cold.

Preheat the oven to 200°C (400°F).

Transfer the stewed fruit to a baking dish. Pour the reserved 250 ml (8½ fl oz/1 cup) stewing liquid over the fruit. Sprinkle the crumble mixture evenly over the top.

Bake for 15–20 minutes, or until the fruit mixture is bubbling and the crumble is brown. Serve warm, with ice cream.

STICKY DATE CAKE WITH SALTED CARAMEL SAUCE AND BURNT SUGAR FIGS

Inspired by Donna Hay's sticky date pudding recipe, which I've been making for crowds for years, this cake has all the comfort of the original, plus a little extra pizzazz. The recipe is incredibly easy and requires no beaters or fancy equipment. Serving the cake warm is a must, with a dollop of cream or good-quality ice cream. The burnt sugar figs add a classy and delicious touch, but pears or banana would also be lovely if figs aren't in season.

———— Makes one 22 cm (8¾ inch) cake • gluten-free option, leftovers friendly ————

INGREDIENTS:

300 g (10½ oz) pitted dates, chopped

405 ml (13½ fl oz/1⅔ cups) hot water

1½ tsp bicarbonate of soda (baking soda)

150 g (5½ oz) salted butter, chopped and softened

230 g (8 oz/1 cup) brown sugar

1 tsp natural vanilla extract

3 eggs

225 g (8 oz/1½ cups) self-raising flour (or gluten-free flour)

Salted Caramel Sauce

345 g (12 oz/1½ cups) brown sugar

150 g (5½ oz) salted butter

250 ml (8½ fl oz/1 cup) pouring (single/light) cream

1 tsp natural vanilla extract

1 tsp sea salt flakes

Figs

25 g (1 oz) butter

3 tbsp brown sugar

4 fresh figs, quartered

METHOD:

Preheat the oven to 170°C (340°F). Line a 22 cm (8¾ inch) round cake tin with baking paper.

Combine the dates and hot water in a large saucepan and bring to the boil. Allow the dates to boil for 2 minutes. Add the bicarbonate of soda and mix well to combine, then allow the mixture to sit for 2–3 minutes. Add the butter, sugar and vanilla and mix well until the butter has completely melted.

Transfer the date mixture to a large mixing bowl and allow to cool down for about 5 minutes. Add the eggs and flour and stir until combined.

Pour the mixture into the cake tin and bake for 1 hour, or until cooked through.

Meanwhile, make the caramel sauce. Put the sugar in a small saucepan over medium heat. When the sugar begins to melt, add the butter, cream and vanilla and whisk well to combine. Bring the mixture to a simmer, then reduce the heat and cook slowly for a few minutes. Turn off the heat, then add the sea salt and mix well. Set the sauce aside.

To prepare the figs, place the butter and sugar in a non-stick frying pan over medium heat and cook for 2 minutes, whisking. Add the figs, cut side down, and cook for 1–2 minutes, or until golden. Remove the sugary figs from the pan and set aside on a plate.

When the cake is cooked, remove from the oven. While it's still hot in the tin, pour a few spoonfuls of the caramel sauce over the cake.

Remove the cake from the tin and allow to cool slightly, then transfer to a serving plate. Pour over more caramel sauce, reserving some for adding to individual serving portions. Arrange the figs on top of the cake and serve.

PEANUT BUTTER AND HONEY BROWNIES

Peanut butter and honey on toast was my comfort breakfast and snack of choice as a kid, and it's still a flavour combination I adore now. These brownies are incredible: the perfect pick-me-up or treat for someone you love. Cook a lot—everyone will want some.

Makes 20 brownies • gluten-free option, leftovers friendly, freezer friendly

INGREDIENTS:

200 g (7 oz) crunchy peanut butter

3 tbsp milk

2 tbsp honey

225 g (8 oz/1½ cups) plain (all-purpose) flour, or 200 g (7 oz/2 cups) almond meal

1 tsp baking powder

90 g (3 oz/¾ cup) good-quality cocoa powder

100 g (3½ oz) butter, softened

125 ml (4 fl oz/½ cup) vegetable oil

345 g (12 oz/1½ cups) caster (superfine) sugar

165 g (6 oz/¾ cup) brown sugar

2 tsp natural vanilla extract

4 eggs

150 g (5½ oz/1 cup) dark chocolate chunks or chips

½ tsp sea salt flakes

METHOD:

Preheat the oven to 180°C (350°F). Line a large baking dish with baking paper.

Put the peanut butter, milk and honey in a small saucepan over low heat. Stir gently to combine, until the mixture becomes thick and a little darker. Turn off the heat and set aside.

Mix the flour, baking powder and cocoa together in a bowl.

In a large bowl, beat together the butter, vegetable oil, caster sugar and brown sugar for 2–4 minutes, or until thick and pale. Add the vanilla, then beat in the eggs one at a time, beating well after each addition.

Add the flour mixture and gently stir until just combined, then fold the chocolate chips through.

Pour the batter into the lined baking dish. Spoon the peanut butter mixture over the top, swirling it to distribute evenly. Sprinkle the sea salt flakes on top.

Bake for 25–30 minutes, or until the batter is just set and no longer wobbly. Be careful not to overcook, to ensure the brownies have a fudgy consistency.

Allow to cool before slicing the brownies. Best eaten fresh, with a cold glass of milk.

ACKNOWLEDGEMENTS

THIS BOOK WAS MADE POSSIBLE BY THE INCREDIBLE SUPPORT AND ASSISTANCE PROVIDED BY SO MANY WONDERFUL FRIENDS, FAMILY MEMBERS AND STRANGERS.

First of all, thank you to Savannah van der Niet, who made this book the beautiful piece of work it is now. Your endless calm, creativity and kindness have balanced my often chaotic and shambolic ideas throughout this process, and I am so grateful to have you as my partner making this book.

To Issy FitzSimons-Reilly, my oldest, dearest friend and housemate. Thank you for your many hours of op-shopping, creating, and sourcing beautiful things to make these images so wonderful. Thank you for being my constant sounding board, kitchen hand and advisor. This book would be nowhere near as beautiful without you. Thank you for making sure I did it properly.

Monika Correa, thank you for contributing your eye and skill in helping to style the book, creating my website and for your ongoing guidance and support in so many endeavours.

Jackson, thank you for your support of this project from day dot, for your ongoing input and logistical guidance, and for your care and belief in me. Thank you for washing dishes, creating so many spreadsheets, talking me through every setback and calming many a meltdown.

A very special thank you to everyone who helped me edit the book. Thank you to my brother Jack, for being so excited by my ideas and supportive of me and my love of cooking from well before this book came into conception. Thank you for your many hours of editing guidance all the way from Halifax, Canada. A very warm thank you to Cassie Dimitroff and Allie Speers. Your voices and input were so vital in ensuring this book reads well and I am so appreciative of your time and skills.

Thank you to all of you who tested recipes and provided valuable feedback and insight. Your generous help improved this book immensely.

To everyone who let me into their home to shoot a chapter of this book, thank you so much. I'm endlessly inspired by sharehouses and the unique and special communities we create in them, and I was fortunate enough to be welcomed into some of the best.

Cookbooks are all about values. Mine have been passed on to me by my wonderful family, both immediate and extended. These are the people who ingrained in me the importance of traditions and rituals around shared meals and strong communities. Thank you to each and every one of you, and a very special thank you to my Mum, Caro, my Dad, Gil and my siblings, Jack, Elly and Hannah for your love and support of this project and of me.

I couldn't have created this book without almost two hundred incredible friends, family and strangers who bought copies before I had even written a single word. Thank you to everyone who supported my crowdfunder in our first print edition.

Thank you Paul and the team at Smith Street Books for believing in the book from its earliest incarnations. As a first timer, your support and guidance have been invaluable, and I'm so appreciative of your help in ensuring *The Shared Table* can find its home in kitchens across the world.

Finally, a very special thank you to my housemates: Issy, Harry, Mon, Fynn, Rose and Ella. Thank you also for graciously putting up with a messy kitchen far more often than you should have to. Above anything, thank you for your friendship, companionship and love. The homes and communities we've created inspired this book.

MAKERS

EVERY SINGLE PROP USED IN THESE PHOTOS WAS SOURCED FROM SECOND-HAND SHOPS OR WAS HANDMADE BY A LOCAL MAKER.

A warm and heartfelt thank you to all the incredible artists who lent us their pottery to shoot with:

<u>Two Warm Hands</u> (Miya Valmadre-McCrae)
twowarmhands.com
Chapters 3, 4 and 5

<u>Kinkfolk & Co.</u>
kinfolkandco.com
Chapters 1 and 3

<u>A Ceramics</u> (Anna Markey)
aceramics.com.au
Chapter 6

<u>Norton & Norton</u> (Jo Norton)
nortonandnorton.com.au
Chapter 7

<u>Holly Hayes</u>
Chapter 4

Woodwork by <u>Issy FitzSimons-Reilly</u> (@issyfitzsimons) is featured throughout

INDEX

INDEX

INDEX

INDEX

Published in 2019 by Smith Street Books
Collingwood | Melbourne | Australia
smithstreetbooks.com

ISBN: 978-1-925811-24-7

Publisher (trade edition): Paul McNally
Design and layout: Savannah van der Niet /
www.savvycreative.com.au / @savvyv
Cover design: Michelle Mackintosh
Food stylist: Clare Scrine
Prop stylists: Issy FitzSimons-Reilly (chapters 2–6 and 8)
and Monika Correa (chapters 1 and 7)
Editors: Jack Scrine, Cassandra Dimitroff, Allie Speers,
Jackson Lapsley Scott and Katri Hilden

Printed & bound in China by C&C Offset Printing Co., Ltd.

Book 102
10 9 8 7 6 5 4 3 2 1